Introduction

This book was born out of a simple yet powerful belief: women can build businesses that honor who we are, our passions, values, and voices, without sacrificing the lives we dream of.

When I first stepped into entrepreneurship, it wasn't because everything was easy or perfectly planned. Like many of you, I faced transitions, challenges, and moments of uncertainty. But what I discovered along the way is this: every setback can be a setup for something greater, and every skill we carry is a seed for opportunity.

The *Biz Her Way Collaborative Playbook* brings together the wisdom of women and men who've walked that very path. Each co-author has poured their story, strategies, and hard-won lessons into these pages. This is not just a book; it's a collective blueprint for creating, growing, and scaling businesses with clarity, courage, and authenticity.

I hope that as you read, you don't just find advice, you find yourself. Your story. Your possibilities. And a reminder that you are not alone on this journey.

Let this playbook be your guide, your encouragement, and your spark as you build business *your way.*

Sacha Walton-Gutierrez, Founder, Biz Her Way

Chapter 1

E.V.O.L.V.E.™ – The Strategic Path to Sustainable Growth

By: Sacha Walton

My journey into entrepreneurship didn't begin with a perfectly mapped-out plan but it began with a bold decision. After years of working in corporate and producing high-level events, I found myself craving something more aligned with my purpose. I stepped into business ownership fueled by passion and drive, but like many women entrepreneurs, I quickly realized passion alone wouldn't cut it. I had the vision, but I needed structure. I needed strategy. I needed a business that could grow with me and not one that drained me.

Over time, I saw a pattern not just in my journey, but in the stories of the women I served. Brilliant women were building brands and launching offers, but they weren't creating businesses that could sustain visibility, manage growth, or scale profits. They were visible, but not profitable. They were busy, but not building with intention. That's when I knew something had to shift.

As a business strategist, I work with women entrepreneurs across various industries, from startups to seasoned CEOs. The one thing they all need is what I call strategic alignment: connecting business development, brand visibility, and marketing into one ecosystem that actually works. That's where the E.V.O.L.V.E.™ Method was born.

The Missing Link Between Your Brilliance and Your Bank Account: Visibility That Converts

You can have the best offer, the best story, and the best intentions, but if no one knows who you are, your business will stay invisible. That's a hard truth many brilliant entrepreneurs face every day.

You post. You tweak your branding. You follow the trends. But the clients? The recognition? The consistent income? They're still inconsistent at best—and non-existent at worst.

What if it's not your content or your offer holding you back?
What if it's your visibility system?

The Real Problem: Visibility Without Strategy

Right now, you may be doing all the 'right things':
- Posting on social media
- Creating reels
- Showing up on live video
- Even pitching yourself

But you're not being strategic, you're being reactive.
Visibility without alignment leads to burnout, confusion, and slow growth.

You don't need more hustle. You need a clear framework that connects visibility to business goals, credibility, and long-term growth.

Introducing the E.V.O.L.V.E.™ Method

The E.V.O.L.V.E.™ Framework is my signature method for helping women entrepreneurs grow with strategy, confidence, and sustainability. It's not just a checklist, but it's a full-circle approach that connects who you are with how you build, show up, and scale. It stands for: Establish, Visualize, Optimize, Leverage, Value, and Elevate.

Let me give you a taste of what that looks like in action, just enough to get you thinking about your next step:

• E – **Establish Your Authority:** Get clear on who you are, what you offer, and why it matters. Without a strong foundation, visibility means nothing.
• V – **Visualize Your Brand Strategy:** Develop a brand that communicates trust, connection, and value before you ever say a word.
• O – **Optimize Your Marketing & Offers:** Market the transformation, not the process. Align your offers with what your audience actually needs.
• L – **Leverage Digital Tools & Platforms:** Automate, streamline, and scale using the right tech and tools—not just trends.
• V – **Value Your Worth:** Price with confidence. Position your brand and offers to reflect the true value you deliver.
• E – **Elevate Through Visibility & Leadership:** It's time to step into the spotlight through media, partnerships, and platforms that expand your influence.

I created this method because I've been where you are. I know what it's like to work hard but feel like something is still missing. You're doing all the things posting, branding, and even selling, but it's not leading to consistent growth. That's because real success comes from alignment, not just activity.
If that resonates with you, then I invite you to take the next step: book an E.V.O.L.V.E.™ Strategy Session with me. In just one call, we'll map out a growth and visibility plan tailored to your business. It's not just about clarity—it's about creating a system that works for you, not against you.

Action Steps to Implement Now
1. Identify Your Business Goal: What is your top priority right now? Is it revenue, reach, or retention? Be clear about your focus.

2. Audit Your Visibility: Google yourself. Review your IG bio, website, and content. Do they reflect your current business and authority?

3. Clarify Your Offer: Can you describe what you sell and the transformation it provides in one sentence? If not, revisit your messaging.

4. Choose One Platform to Own: Pick one platform to show up on consistently for the next 30 days. Build momentum with focus, not chaos.

5. Book a Strategy Call: If you're ready for aligned growth and sustainable visibility, schedule a strategy session and let's create your custom roadmap.

You don't need more tactics, you need strategy. You don't need to do more you need to evolve. Your next level is waiting, but it requires a new version of you. Let's build that version together.

About The Visionary Author

Sacha Walton is a dynamic business strategist, speaker, and CEO of SWI Management Group, known for helping women entrepreneurs scale with strategy, sustainability, and soul. She is the visionary force behind *Biz Her Way™* a platform, summit, and publication spotlighting bold women in business who are disrupting norms and rewriting the rules. With a background in government contracting and a proven track record of empowering founders, creatives, and professionals, Sacha fuses data-driven strategy with heart-centered leadership.

Her signature E.V.O.L.V.E.™ framework guides women in building legacy businesses rooted in clarity, confidence, and connection. Sacha is also the founder and developer of MoolaFox™, AI CFO an AI powered financial management ecosystem. She has been featured in **Forbes, Essence, GoBankingRates, Valiant CEO**, and **American Express Business**, sharing insights on entrepreneurship, financial empowerment, and inclusive leadership. She was also highlighted by the **CO Chamber of Commerce** in a feature on government contracting and small business success. Sacha isn't just building brands — she's cultivating movements.

www.swimgtgroup.com

Facebook & LinkedIn: Sacha Walton | Instagram: ThatGirlSach

Chapter 2

The Invisible Marketer:

How AI Helped Me Reclaim Time, Grow Faster, and Stay Ahead

By: Maribel Sanabria

There was a time when I felt like I was doing everything—and somehow still falling behind.

As a single mother of three and the founder of a growing marketing business, my days were a blur of client meetings, late-night proposal writing, and the chaotic ballet of school drop-offs, sports practices, and surprise science projects. I was exhausted, constantly chasing the next thing on my to-do list, and quietly wondering: *Is this what success is supposed to feel like?*

I didn't need more motivation. I was scrambling to keep my head above water and I needed more time.
Instead, I found something better—Artificial Intelligence.

Running a business while raising three children alone and still working a 9-5 meant juggling the impossible, often with one hand while the other cooked dinner or drafted social captions. I loved my work, but the truth was hard to ignore: I didn't have the bandwidth to do it strategically. I was stuck in survival mode, constantly reacting instead of leading.

Marketing felt like an uphill climb with no summit in sight. Social media changed daily. SEO strategies evolved overnight. Clients expected personalization and speed, but I barely had time to respond to emails. Things were slipping fast. I didn't just need help—I needed leverage.

At the time, AI sounded like a buzzword reserved for tech startups and corporations with innovation departments. It certainly didn't sound like something a stretched-thin solopreneur could lean on. But burnout has a funny way of opening your mind. One late night, in a fog of exhaustion and frustration, I gave an AI writing assistant a try; ChatGpt to the rescue.

Within minutes, it drafted a version of a blog post I had been procrastinating on for a week. I blinked. Refined. Added some personal touches. In less than half an hour, it was ready to go.

That moment changed everything for me.

Once I saw what AI could do with content, I turned my attention to SEO. I began exploring platforms like SurferSEO and Clearscope tools that analyze top-performing pages and recommend the keywords, structure, and tone needed to rank competitively. What used to take me hours of research, comparison, and blind guessing was now data-backed and delivered in minutes. This was the start of something truly amazing and I began to feel like I could breathe again.

Instead of trying to keep up with Google's shifting algorithm, I let AI guide me. I optimized existing blog posts, restructured service pages, and created new content based on actual demand and intent. I wasn't just publishing more I was publishing smarter and gaining traction with my target audience.

Within weeks, my organic traffic saw measurable improvement. But what mattered most? I did it without burning out.

Traffic is only part of the equation. You can bring in an audience, but without engagement and conversion, it's just noise. That's where AI-driven personalization became my secret weapon and I began to deploy.

I implemented a chatbot using ManyChat a tool that required no coding and very little time to set up. What started as a simple lead capture assistant evolved into a round-the-clock client concierge. It answered common questions, directed users to the right services, and even delivered customized offers. All while I was off the clock, living my life and being present with my kids.

It wasn't just the chatbot. I began using AI-powered tools to segment audiences and send tailored follow-up emails. I built custom gpt's that performed targeted services within my business essentially creating a workforce without increasing my overhead. Then, I created dynamic landing pages that adjusted to user behavior. Conversion rates rose, bounce rates dropped, and client satisfaction improved all without expanding my team or adding hours to my day.

Before AI, much of my energy went to repetitive, low-impact tasks: formatting newsletters, repurposing content for social media, resizing graphics, managing schedules. Important, yes—but draining.

With automation tools like Zapier and Buffer, paired with generative AI like Jasper and ChatGpt, I created systems that took care of the busywork. AI now helps me brainstorm headlines, test copy variations, and even generate content outlines for client campaigns.

This gave me back something priceless: time to think. Time to reflect. Time to innovate.

I began investing that time into learning. Following trends. Sharpening my creative instincts. That shift from tactical operator to strategic leader has been the single most transformative outcome of embracing AI in my business.

The biggest surprise? It wasn't just about ROI or metrics. It was about the human moments AI made possible.

Like the time I was able to say yes to attending every single one of my child's ball games without having a laptop on standby, knowing the chatbot was handling lead inquiries. Or the Saturday I didn't work and decided to focus on some much needed self-care because automated email campaigns were already queued and optimized.

These moments reminded me that success isn't just about doing more. It's about doing the right things, in less time, with less stress, and with more joy.

You don't need to overhaul your business overnight. AI isn't all-or-nothing. It's incremental and incredibly forgiving.

If you're curious where to begin, start with what drains you. Choose one repetitive task like writing captions or scheduling posts and test an AI tool to streamline it. Update one piece of content. Use an SEO assistant to refresh an old blog post or service page and watch how it performs. Add one automation. Whether it's a chatbot or an email sequence, find one spot to let technology take the wheel.

None of these require you to be a tech wizard. They just require a willingness to try.

AI didn't replace me. It revealed the version of me that had been buried under to-do lists and time constraints. It showed me that I didn't need more hours—I needed better tools. And most importantly, it helped me step out of the role of invisible marketer and into the role of visible, empowered CEO.

To anyone else who's wearing too many hats and wondering if it's possible to do more with less: it is.

AI won't solve everything. But it will give you space to grow, to lead, to breathe. And sometimes, that's all you really need.

About The Author

Maribel Sanabria is the CEO and founder of Grafically Yours, a company specializing in innovative solutions that combine creativity, technology, and strategy. With expertise in digital graphic design, marketing, branding, and AI consulting, she helps businesses and individuals streamline processes, amplify their brand, and achieve sustainable growth. Passionate about making an impact, Maribel tailors her approach to meet each client's unique needs, ensuring measurable outcomes and alignment with their vision. Believing that creativity and technology are tools for both professional and personal growth, Maribel empowers clients to reclaim their time and focus on what matters most. As she says, "Time is the canvas, efficiency is the brush—paint the life you've always wanted!"

www.graficallyyours.com
Facebook & Instagram: Grafically Yours | LinkedIn: Maribel Sanabria

Chapter 3

Standing On My Own Two Feet:

Helping others turn Pain Into Purpose into Passion into Power into Profit
By: Lemika Early

My name is Lemika Early, and I am a **Mobility Motivational Speaker**, a 5-star **Published Author**, **Mentor**, **Business Owner** of Poetic Angels, Mother, and a survivor who turned tragedy into triumph. But before all the titles and achievements, I was a 14-year-old girl in a coma, declared dead three times, holding on to life by a thread until God whispered, *"Not yet. I'm not done with you."*

That moment reshaped everything.

"When life broke my body, faith rebuilt my vision." 6. **"Confidence is the voice that spoke louder than the doctor's prognosis."** After the car accident that left me paralyzed, I could've given up. In fact, many expected I would. Doctors said, I'd never walk again. Some friends disappeared. at times, even my hope went missing. But what I discovered through pain, prayer, and persistence was that you don't have to stand on your feet to stand in your power.

I learned to mentally stand and that made all the difference.

My Entrepreneurial Journey: Built From the Ground Up

They say necessity is the mother of invention. In my case, pain was the mother of purpose. I had two choices: sink into silence or speak life into others.

So I started speaking, sharing my testimony, my tears, my truth. From local church events to Toastmasters, from open mics to boardrooms, I brought *"Standing On My Own Two Feet"* everywhere I went. But more importantly, I brought people with me. Mothers in pain. Survivors of loss. Young people on the edge. Disabled individuals who felt invisible.

What started as storytelling became a **brand**. What began as inspiration became a **business**. Today, I proudly operate as a **Mobility Motivational Speaker**, offering workshops, books, one-on-one sessions, and keynote speeches that remind people: *Your setback is a setup for a stronger comeback.*

I didn't do it blindly. I did it intentionally with **structure**, strategy, and soul.

My Framework: Six Steps That Saved My Life

Here's the framework I not only teach but live by. These six daily habits became my blueprint for *mobility and motivation,* even when I couldn't move physically. They restored my mindset, stabilized my emotions, and launched my business. I call it my **Mobility Mindset Remedy**:

> 1. **Meditation**
> Each day, I begin with stillness. I listen to God. I check in with Lemika. In a noisy world, silence is a

superpower. Meditation gives me clarity before chaos creeps in. Whether it's five minutes or fifteen, this practice grounds me.

2. Minding My Business
Literally and figuratively. I don't have time to compete or compare. I've got purpose to protect. Minding my business means focusing on my lane—my healing, my hustle, my goals. It's about protecting your energy and refusing to be distracted by what doesn't serve you.

3. Structure
Success needs a schedule. As a mother and entrepreneur, I need flow and flexibility—but also discipline. I map out my day, assign time to tasks, and block space for rest. Structure keeps me accountable to my dream.

4. Confidence
I had to learn that confidence doesn't mean I have all the answers and it means I trust myself to find them. Wheelchair or not, I enter rooms with my head high and my spirit higher. I walk by faith, not by fear.

5. Positivity
Optimism isn't naïve, it's necessary. I look for the light, even in dark seasons. Positivity is a choice I make daily, especially when life gets heavy. I don't fake it;
I *fight* for it.

6. Doing Good Deeds
Serving others is healing. I use my voice, my story, and my time to uplift people. Whether it's a motivational

call, a shared meal, or simply a smile, I plant seeds. That's how I stay in momentum. That's how I rise.

Every story I share is a hand extended to someone else climbing out of despair. I serve by being real. Raw. Unfiltered. I don't pretend it's easy, but I prove it's possible.

Through my **book**, *A Letter From An Angel*, I open the door for healing. Through my **poem**, *Standing On My Own Two Feet*, I offer strength to the silent sufferer. Through my **speaking engagements**, I guide others from hopelessness to hope.

But it's not just talk. I provide **actionable strategies** for mental, emotional, and entrepreneurial mobility. I help people:
- Build a mindset that won't break under pressure
- Create structure in chaos
- Start purpose-driven projects with confidence
- Turn pain into purpose and profit
- Find healing and meaning in their journey

From single moms struggling to find time for themselves, to young adults battling low self-worth, to entrepreneurs starting with nothing, I serve those ready to **rise**.

Key Takeaways: How You Can Start Today
1. **Your story matters.**
Don't bury your pain—build with it. Your testimony might be the key to someone else's breakthrough.
2. **Use what you have.**
I didn't wait for perfect conditions. I started with what I had—my voice, my story, and my will. That was enough.

3. **Be consistent with your six steps.**
Every day, practice your version of my six-step remedy.
These habits transform not just your mood, but your
momentum.
4. **Stop shrinking.**
You've survived too much to play small. Confidence
isn't arrogance, it's obedience to the gift God gave you.
5. **Do good.**
Serving others is not just a blessing to them—it's
healing for you. The more you give, the more you
grow.

Final Words

I may be in a wheelchair, but my spirit *runs free*. I've built a
business, a brand, and a beautiful life not in spite of my tragedy,
but *because of it*. That's what mobility is about. It's not about
walking it's about *moving forward*.

So, if you're reading this and feel stuck, broken, or lost let me
remind you:

You can stand again.
You can speak again.
You can build again.
You can *live again.*

All it takes is one step.
Let's take it together.

About The Author

Lemika Early is a Mobility Motivational Speaker, published author, and CEO of Poetic Angels LLC. At just 14 years old, she survived a devastating car crash that left her paralyzed and in a coma—but it also awakened her purpose. Declared dead three times, Lemika defied the odds and chose to live with intention. From her wheelchair, she built a powerful voice that now helps others mentally "Stand On Their Own Two Feet."

She developed the 6 Mobility Motivational Remedies for Success: Meditation, Minding My Business, Structure, Confidence, Positivity, and Doing Good Deeds—daily habits that helped her rebuild her life. A Toastmasters leader and mother, Lemika uses poetry, personal testimony, and raw truth to uplift those facing adversity. Her story reminds us that tragedy can spark triumph, and purpose has no limits. Today, she empowers people with disabilities, single mothers, and anyone stuck in survival mode to rise with resilience.

Facebook & LinkedIn: Lemika Early

Chapter 4

The 5 Love Languages in Business

By: Jerreme Wade

Originally introduced by Dr. Gary Chapman to improve romantic relationships, the 5 Love Languages hold unexpected power in the business world, especially for women. In professional settings, women often navigate complexities emotionally. Self-love, self-care, and self-worth can be overlooked, yet they are critical for success. When embraced, love languages help strengthen teams, elevate leadership, and deepen client relationships. This chapter explores how these languages can be reimagined as tools for professional empowerment.

Why Love Languages Matter in Business

Love, in business, doesn't mean emotional vulnerability in the traditional sense, but it implies intentionality, empathy, and connection. Women who lead with care and purpose often foster more effective collaborations. By understanding how love languages shape communication and action, women can model leadership rooted in authenticity and purpose. When you lead with love, it shows in your words, presence, and results.

1. Words of Affirmation → Encouragement

In business, words matter. Encouragement uplifts morale, reinforces value, and affirms purpose. For women, especially in male-dominated industries, positive affirmation combats imposter syndrome and helps cultivate confidence.

Use Words of Affirmation to:

- Recognize effort and insight ("Your ideas in that meeting were valuable.")
- Publicly celebrate achievements

- Offer sincere feedback that affirms growth

Leadership Tip: Audit your leadership language. Are your words affirming your team or merely managing them? Today, rewrite one email or message with intentional encouragement. Regularly affirm your team. Likewise, invite feedback that acknowledges your own contributions. Encouragement isn't just emotional, it's strategic.

2. Physical Touch → Hugs and Handshakes

In business, appropriate physical gestures such as handshakes and occasional hugs can signal respect, trust, and shared success. A firm handshake or brief hug can seal deals and strengthen rapport.

Use Physical Touch to:

- Build trust through professional gestures
- Celebrate milestones or long-standing partnerships
- Offer grounding presence in high-stress moments

Leadership Tip: At your next meeting or event, focus on presence, offer a handshake, eye contact, or meaningful gesture to build a connection. Rely on emotional intelligence to assess when these gestures are appropriate. Even eye contact and body language count as physical affirmations of connection.

3. Quality Time → Networking & Collaboration

Spending focused time with clients, colleagues, and peers builds deeper professional relationships. Women thrive in collaborative, supportive environments, mentorship, masterminds, and shared projects.

Use Quality Time to:

- Foster brainstorming and innovation

- Build mentorship relationships
- Encourage meaningful dialogue beyond surface-level transactions

Leadership Tip: Block 30 minutes this week for a quality conversation with a peer, mentee, or collaborator. Make space for growth through connection. Host a co-working sessions or intentional meetups. Creating relational and not just transactional experiences nurtures long-term growth.

4. Gifts → Results & Deliverables

In business, the "gifts" are the tangible results of your work projects being completed, problems solved, and services delivered. These outcomes serve as evidence of your excellence and commitment.

Use Gifts to:

- Demonstrate value through high-quality work
- Surprise clients with thoughtful tokens of appreciation
- Reinforce your brand promise through delivery

Leadership Tip: Treat your next deliverable like a personal gift finished with excellence Let your work speak for your integrity, creativity, and expertise.

5. Acts of Service → Responsibilities

Business success thrives on reliability. Acts of service in this context are about showing up, fulfilling responsibilities, and being willing to support others when needed.

Use Acts of Service to:

- Go above and beyond in your role
- Support peers through challenges
- Handle tasks that ease the burden on others

Leadership Tip: Identify one way to support a colleague today. Offer help, lighten their load, emotional support, administrative coordination, team morale boosting or acknowledge their invisible labor. Responsibility is love in action.

Integrating Love into Leadership

When women apply love languages professionally, they foster cultures of empathy, trust, and mutual support. These languages encourage emotionally intelligent leadership that:

- Deepens relationships
- Increases team synergy
- Builds trust and loyalty
- Prevents burnout through shared support

A successful woman in business uplifts others, creates safe spaces for dialogue, and leads with both strength and compassion.

Final Thoughts

Business doesn't have to be cold or transactional. It can be a heart-centered space where love shows up in how we collaborate, communicate, and lead. The 5 Love Languages offer a framework for intentional, relational business practices that elevate everyone involved.

As women rise in entrepreneurship and leadership, integrating emotional intelligence into business becomes essential. Let your language reflect your love for your work, your collaborators, and yourself. You can achieve far more than just the bottom line.

About The Author

Jerreme Wade, a passionate and expert writer who turns complex concepts into clear and concise copy. 2012 Paralympian and member of the US Soccer Team.

Instagram: JerremeCW

Chapter 5

The Power of Passion: Balancing Leadership and Self-Care
By: Natalie Boehm

As entrepreneurs, staying focused on our goals and taking the necessary steps to achieve them can be challenging. Emotions often come into play, making the journey both exciting and demanding.

One of the strongest emotions entrepreneurs experience is passion. According to the Cambridge Dictionary (2025), passion is a feeling or expression of strong emotions, beliefs, or convictions. Entrepreneurs are deeply passionate about their work, often making their business their entire life. However, many neglect self-care, relationships, and overall well-being in pursuit of success.

I was guilty of all the above. For years, I worked seven days a week, believing I was setting a positive example for my team. I was determined to stay ahead, to lead by example, and to be the driving force behind my company. However, I unknowingly did the opposite. I took on tasks that should have been delegated, struggled with trust issues, and believed that no one could execute my vision as I could. Though I did not micromanage, I failed to allow my team the opportunity to prove themselves, learn, and grow.

The result was devastating. I experienced burnout, depression, and exhaustion. Not long after, I was diagnosed with early-stage breast cancer. My life took a drastic turn, forcing me to prioritize my health. I had no choice but to take care of myself and, for the first time, admit that I needed help while recovering from surgery.

Sending an email to my team about my diagnosis was painful, but it was necessary. In meeting with them, I guided them in setting goals to manage responsibilities during my recovery. It was then that I realized their capabilities and the importance of trusting them to take on greater roles.

During my recovery from a bilateral mastectomy, I reflected on the changes I needed to make. The first step was forgiving myself for past neglect. Next, I committed to setting new goals for self-care and ensuring I did not fall back into old habits. I feared failing at this, so I created a plan to hold myself accountable.

The first change was structuring my schedule to include breaks. Whether for journaling, meditating, gardening, or walking, these moments became non-negotiable wellness time. During these breaks, I was unavailable for work-related tasks, ensuring I prioritized my well-being. Since adopting this approach, my work has improved, my self-awareness and emotional intelligence have strengthened, and I feel genuinely happier. Investing in myself has made me stronger both personally and professionally.

Another crucial change was learning to say no. Leaders strive to achieve their goals, set examples, and push forward. However, taking on too much makes success unattainable. As someone passionate about nonprofit work, helping others brings me joy. Yet, I cannot commit to every project or collaboration. When I started saying no, some were surprised, while others became frustrated. Those who could not respect my boundaries were individuals I chose to no longer work with. If someone cannot acknowledge that I am human and have limitations, I do not have the capacity to engage with that level of toxicity.

Here are five steps you can take to achieve self-care:

1. Make time in your day to do something for you. Whether it is going to a yoga session, meditating, having coffee with a friend, a spa day, reward yourself with something. You cannot lead a team until you take care of yourself.

2. Work to establish trust with your team and learn to give up control. Many type A professionals have a hard time giving up

control. You need to allow your team to work on their goals and help you take things to the next level. Allow them the opportunity to do so.

3. Do not be afraid to say no. You cannot do everything. Be smart when it comes to what you are taking on and if you cannot contribute to something, there is nothing wrong in stepping back. The last thing you want to do is burnout.

4. Acknowledge to yourself that you are human, you cannot do everything. Set realistic goals to achieve what you need to do. You don't have to be a superhero.

5. Focus on your overall wellness and take care of yourself. Wellness is more than physical wellness. Emotional and mental wellness are just as important. Seeking help from a therapist if needed is important. Don't worry about what others think; your wellbeing matters. Focus on taking care of yourself.

Ultimately, self-care must come first. Passion is a powerful force, but it must be directed wisely. Passion alone will not lead to success unless it includes a commitment to personal well-being. We are our strongest advocates, and as professionals, we must set realistic goals and prioritize ourselves in order to thrive.

Resources:
Cambridge Dictionary (2025). Meaning of Passionate in English. Cambridge Dictionary. Retrieved from:
https://dictionary.cambridge.org/us/dictionary/english/passionate

About The Author
Natalie Boehm is an entrepreneur, author, public speaker, and disability advocate committed to creating meaningful change. As the president of The Defeating Epilepsy Foundation, she leverages her expertise in advocacy, nonprofit leadership, and organizational development to

improve the lives of individuals with chronic illnesses. Having battled epilepsy for most of her life, Natalie understands firsthand the challenges of navigating healthcare and insurance systems.

Her work focuses on reducing stigma, advocating for better healthcare access, and fostering collaboration among organizations to drive positive change. Passionate about ensuring dignity and respect for those with chronic conditions, she is dedicated to empowering the next generation to live without the discrimination many before them have faced. Through her leadership, Natalie continues to challenge barriers and create opportunities for those in need, making a lasting impact on the chronic illness and disability communities.

www.defeatingepilepsy.org
LinkedIn: Natalie Aswad Boehm

Chapter 6

From Burnout to Breakthrough: Building Biz My Way

By Ammie Michaels

I didn't leave corporate to be exhausted again.

But there I was staring at my laptop, paralyzed by a to-do list that never ended, wondering why the business I created out of passion had become something I resented. I'd dreamed of freedom. Flexibility. Purpose. But the reality? I was drowning in pressure I had placed on myself.

The truth is, no one really talks about this part of entrepreneurship.

The part where your dream business starts to feel like a trap. The part where success looks good on the outside but feels suffocating on the inside. The part where you've built something but you're not even sure you want it anymore.

I thought burnout was something I left behind in my 9-to-5 days. But I quickly realized burnout has a way of sneaking into entrepreneurship too, especially when you carry your old patterns into your new business.

The Burnout No One Talks About

I had said yes to everything: every opportunity, every client, every request, because I believed that's what "building a business" required. I wore every hat: marketer, operations, admin, visionary, customer service, HR (of course). I gave everything to the business, but somewhere along the way, I stopped giving anything to myself.

What started as a passion turned into performance. I wasn't just working; I was proving. Proving I could do it. Proving I could replace my income. Proving I was successful.

But inside? I was tired. Not "I need a nap" tired...soul tired.

There were days I felt like a fraud. I was helping other leaders build better teams and cultures, yet behind the scenes, I was falling apart, too proud to ask for help, too overwhelmed to see a way out.

I kept telling myself, "This is just the season I'm in." But the season never ended. And deep down, I knew I hadn't built a business; I'd built another cage.

What Was Really Draining Me

It wasn't the work itself; it was how I was doing it.

I was over-functioning. People-pleasing. Saying yes when I meant no. Letting boundaries blur because I didn't want to disappoint anyone. I was saying "yes" out of fear—fear of missing out, of letting someone down, of not making enough, of being seen as selfish or lazy.

I was operating from survival, not strategy.

I built a schedule that didn't match my energy. I worked late into the night to catch up, telling myself rest was something I'd earn after the next launch, the next win, the next milestone. But rest doesn't wait—it demands attention. And when you ignore it long enough, your body, your creativity, and your spirit begin to shut down.

There was one moment that hit me hard. I had just finished facilitating a leadership workshop—something I normally loved. But instead of feeling energized, I felt nothing. Numb. I remember thinking, If I don't make a change soon, I'm going to lose the spark completely.

That scared me.

I didn't start my business to burn out. I started it to come alive.

The Breakthrough Begins

Breakthroughs rarely show up as big, dramatic events. Mine came in small whispers at first. A journal entry that turned into a truth I couldn't unsee. A therapist session where I admitted I didn't even enjoy half the work I was doing. A moment of stillness that revealed I wasn't just tired—I was misaligned.

The first breakthrough was this: I don't have to run my business like everyone else.

That one thought cracked something open in me.

I started asking better questions:
What would my business look like if it were built around my well-being instead of my worthiness?
What if joy was the goal, not the reward?

It didn't happen overnight. I wrestled with the guilt. The discomfort of letting go of what no longer fit. The fear that simplifying meant shrinking.

But I stayed with it. I chose intention over intensity. I traded validation for alignment.

Rebuilding With Heart (and Systems)

Once I got honest with myself, I started building again, but this time, from a different foundation.

I designed my business around my values: authenticity, emotional intelligence, joy, and connection. I shifted from high-touch services to leveraged offers. I allowed systems and automation to help me breathe again. And I stopped glamorizing the hustle.

I gave myself permission to make joy part of the strategy. Whether it was integrating LEGO into my workshops or choosing clients who felt aligned, I built my way with play, intention, and a lot of unlearning.

I got clearer about who I really wanted to serve and what kind of business I wanted to lead, not just what I was capable of building, but what I actually wanted to experience day-to-day.

I asked for help, something the "old me" would've never done. I found a community of other women doing business differently. And in those relationships, I felt seen. Held. Reminded that I wasn't meant to do this alone.

Burnout taught me what my business needed most: boundaries, belief, and breathing room.

Doing Biz My Way...And Loving It

Here's the truth: I still work hard. But now I work from a place of overflow, not overwhelm.

I've learned that success isn't just about revenue or recognition. It's about waking up and being proud of the life you've built, not just the business.

I've learned that burnout doesn't mean you're broken. It's an invitation to come back home to yourself.

And I've learned that doing business "my way" doesn't mean I have it all figured out. It means I no longer abandon myself trying to fit into someone else's mold.

If you're in that in-between space (somewhere between burnout and breakthrough), I want you to know: you're not alone. You're not weak. You're not behind.

You're just being called into deeper alignment.

Let this be your permission slip to rewrite the rules. To unhook from the "shoulds." To build a business that doesn't just look good but feels good.

That's what Biz Her Way is really about.
That's what my way looks like now.

And I wouldn't trade it for anything.

About The Author

Ammie Michaels is living proof that thoughtful leadership and intentional design can change your life. She brings sharp insight and calm clarity to help others get unstuck and realign with what matters most. Through her consulting firm, WolfpackHR, Ammie empowers individuals to shift their mindset, trust themselves, and create the career or business they actually want.

With a background in HR, conflict resolution, and facilitation, she leads one on one sessions and group workshops that spark meaningful change in teams centered around communication, collaboration, and connection. Her gift lies in seeing all angles, eliminating guesswork, and designing sharp solutions that build trust and prevent problems before they start. Today, she guides others to do the same while running her business from the Black Hills with her husband, their two teens, and two lovable Weimaraners.

www.wolfpackhr.com

Facebook & LinkedIn: Ammie Michaels

Chapter 7

Lead Like an Icon: Your Wardrobe Is Your Hidden Leadership Strategy

By: Bria Johnson

Owning My Worth

I learned early on that how I dressed wasn't just about fashion: it was about owning my worth. My Nana was the epitome of grace, moving through the world with elegance that demanded respect without a single word spoken. Watching her taught me that clothes carry power. They shape how you are seen, and more importantly, how you see yourself.

That truth has followed me from childhood mirrors to boardrooms, from private closets to the platforms where leaders are seen and remembered. And here's what most leaders don't realize: your wardrobe isn't decoration; it's your hidden leadership strategy. It can dilute your presence, or it can amplify your authority, confidence, and clarity.

Why Style is Strategy

Before you've spoken, your image has already delivered the opening statement.
Leadership isn't just what you say: it's how you arrive. In the first seven seconds, people form judgments about your credibility, capacity, and command. Those impressions shape the way they listen, trust, and respond.

When your wardrobe aligns with your goals, everything accelerates: decisions are made faster, doors open with less resistance, and your message lands before you ever say a word.

Style isn't superficial. It's strategic. A wardrobe, when aligned with intention, becomes an asset just as vital as a résumé, a pitch deck, or an executive coach. Done right, it doesn't just dress you; it positions you.

The I.C.O.N.I.C With Style™ Framework

In my work, I've met ambitious women who were powerful in their craft yet caught in the quiet frustration of "I have nothing to wear." The truth? They didn't need more clothes. They needed alignment. With nearly two decades of combined leadership and image consulting experience, I approach style not as fashion, but as a leadership strategy.

That belief led me to create the I.C.O.N.I.C With Style™ Framework: six key steps designed to give women structure, confidence, and clarity in how they present themselves to the world. It's not about shopping more; it's about aligning your image with your ambition so the world sees the leader you already are.

1. **Identify:** Gain clarity on your goals, your identity, and the future self you're stepping into.

2. **Curate:** Edit your wardrobe with intention, removing the "almost right" pieces and choosing only what supports your vision.

3. **Optimize:** Elevate through tailoring, fit, and signature details so your clothes work as hard as you do.

4. **Navigate:** Step boldly into new rooms and opportunities, showing up with the confidence your work deserves.

5. **Integrate:** weave your image strategy into how you show up each day, making confidence a reliable standard, not a passing mood.

6. **Continue:** Sustain long-term presence with refreshes and rituals that evolve as you grow.

The framework is the roadmap. But the transformation begins when your wardrobe stops reflecting where you've been and starts projecting where you're going.

What Transformation Looks Like

When style is treated as strategy, the results go far beyond clothes. Alignment changes everything:

Clarity. A leader's image mirrors her goals, creating instant consistency between who she is and how she's perceived.

Ease. The daily stress of "what do I wear?" disappears, replaced by efficiency and calm.

Presence. The room is quiet when she enters; her image speaks before she does.

Sustainability. Systems and techniques keep her style evolving as her influence and responsibilities grow.

The framework provides the roadmap. But the true power lies in the lived transformation: the shift from "I'm dressed" to "I'm leading."

The Presence Playbook

Your wardrobe is not decoration; it's a leadership instrument. When approached with strategy, it becomes a tool that communicates trust, confidence, and presence before you ever speak.

Here are five strategies to begin experimenting with. They'll give you a taste of what alignment can do, and why style, treated as strategy, changes everything.

The Fit Factor

Nothing communicates authority faster than clothes that fit impeccably. Poor fit dilutes credibility, while tailoring transforms even the simplest piece into a signal of control. Fit isn't detail. It's strategy.

The Power Palette
Choose two neutrals and one signature power color to weave consistently through your wardrobe. A defined palette eliminates decision fatigue, photographs cohesively, and reinforces your brand presence.

The Consistency Rule

Icons are remembered because their image is recognizable. Decide on one signature, whether it's a silhouette, a color, or an accessory, and repeat it often enough that people begin to associate it with you. Repetition builds recognition, and recognition builds influence.

The Leadership Mirror

Your closet should be a reflection, not a museum. If a piece belongs to the woman you used to be, let it go. Create room for the wardrobe of your future self.

The Boardroom Three

For high-stakes moments, ground yourself with three non-negotiables: structure, polish, and one intentional detail. These anchor points ensure your look amplifies your voice instead of competing with it.

These five strategies are just a beginning. True transformation doesn't come from a handful of tips. It comes from alignment, from embedding style into the way you lead, and from building an image that rises with your ambition. Consider this a doorway into what's possible when your style works in service of your goals.

Closing

You don't need more clothes. You need alignment. When your wardrobe reflects your ambition, confidence becomes steady, undeniable, and present. Leaders are remembered for how they make decisions and how they make people feel. Your image does both, quietly and powerfully, every time you enter a room.

So ask yourself this: Am I dressing for the woman I've been, or for the Icon I am becoming?

About The Author

Bria Johnson is the Chief Style Strategist of I.C.O.N.I.C With Style™, where she helps ambitious women align their wardrobe with their goals so they can step fully into their next level. Inspired by her grandmother's elegance and her own journey through leadership, Bria knows that style is more than clothing it's a strategy for influence. With nearly two decades of combined leadership and image consulting experience, she equips her clients to command rooms and embody the Icons they are becoming.

www.iconicwithstyle.com

Instagram: IconicWithStyle

Chapter 8

Closing the Leadership Gap

By: Earl Morrison

Leadership isn't a one-size-fits-all model. The generational gap in leadership is one of the most pressing challenges of today's workforce. Whether you're a seasoned leader or a rising star, the gap in how we lead, communicate, and collaborate is wider than we think. Differences in leadership—across age groups, cultural backgrounds, and experiences shape how organizations grow, evolve, and sometimes, struggle.

From my years as a police chief to transitioning into business, I've seen both the frustration and the opportunities this divide offers. Closing the Gap isn't just theory; it's a practical guide on how leaders, regardless of generation, can come together to create cohesive, effective, and successful teams.

My leadership journey has been shaped by my time in law enforcement and my transition into business, where I faced a growing generational divide. As a police chief, I saw how each generation brought its own approach to leadership, communication, and decision-making. The challenge was uniting officers from different age groups, each with distinct values, experiences, and work ethics. It became clear that the gap wasn't just about age, it was about mindset, communication styles, and views on authority, teamwork, and progress.

When I moved into business, I realized this generational divide wasn't unique to law enforcement. It existed in businesses, communities, and personal relationships. This insight led me to focus on what united us, not just what divided us. I set out to bridge the gap by embracing shared values, fostering respect, and understanding evolving generational dynamics.

Over time, I developed strategies to help leaders navigate these divides, improve communication, and create cultures of collaboration. The key to success lies in embracing these differences to create stronger, more innovative leadership.

Recognizing the Strength of Ego and Character

One of the first lessons I learned in law enforcement was how ego can interfere with effective leadership. Regardless of age or experience, ego clouds judgment and creates barriers in communication, especially across generations. Over time, I learned that the best way to close the generational gap was to set aside my own ego and prioritize the team's needs. Leadership isn't about asserting dominance; it's about serving others and creating an environment where every voice is heard.

As I navigated challenges in both law enforcement and business, I learned that success depends on balancing confidence with humility. By leading with character and tempering ego, I connected with my team on a deeper level, fostering collaboration and driving results.

Foundation Matters: Establishing Core Values That Transcend Generations

When I started building my business, I knew that any leadership program, mentoring initiative, or organizational development strategy had to be grounded in a strong foundation—one that transcended generations. Core values like integrity, accountability, and respect are timeless; they aren't tied to any specific age group. These values provide common ground where all generations can come together.

As I integrated these values into every leadership training program I created, whether for police officers, business professionals, or community leaders, they served as the foundation that bridged generational divides and created alignment. These core principles guide actions, decisions, and behaviors, regardless of when or where you were born. Without shared values, the generational gap becomes too wide to cross, and the cohesion needed for success falters.

Building a strong foundation based on shared values allowed me to create an environment where teams could work in unison, even when generational differences seemed daunting. Integrity, accountability, and respect were not just words; they were the pillars upon which effective leadership rested, helping to foster an environment of collaboration, trust, and unity.

Leading by Example and Mentorship

One of the most powerful tools for bridging generational gaps is mentorship. Leadership isn't just about giving instructions; it's about creating an environment where learning flows both ways. Mentorship isn't just about passing down knowledge; it's an opportunity to understand and learn from those you lead.

I made it a priority to mentor younger leaders, just as I had been mentored. What I discovered is that mentorship is a two-way street. While I shared my experience, younger leaders shared their fresh perspectives, creativity, and tech-savvy approaches with me. This exchange of wisdom and ideas helped me adapt to new ways of thinking, leading to more effective leadership.

Mentorship fosters respect, collaboration, and mutual understanding. By leading by example, I inspired others to continuously grow and develop, not just in terms of tasks, but in how they approach their own growth. Mentorship across generations strengthens teams, allowing leaders to bridge divides, learn from each other, and grow together.

Character Drives Organizational Success

As I moved from law enforcement into business, I was reminded that the most powerful asset a leader can possess isn't just technical expertise or skills, but their character. I had always understood the importance of character throughout my career, but transitioning into business reinforced just how vital it is.

A character-driven organization isn't just focused on getting things done; it's about doing things the right way. Leaders who lead with integrity and build a culture rooted in trust and accountability foster success. A strong character-driven approach builds long-term success by creating a workplace where respect and values are prioritized, ensuring growth and resilience.

A leader's character becomes the foundation of the organization. It shapes how decisions are made, how challenges are approached, and how success is defined. In my law enforcement career, when facing crises or challenges, it was always our integrity, trust, and commitment to doing the right thing that carried us through.

Accountability Across Generations: Holding Ourselves and Each Other to High Standards

Accountability is the cornerstone of any successful organization, and it applies across generations. When I transitioned into business, I was determined to create a culture where accountability was embraced by everyone. In law enforcement, accountability was non-negotiable, and I carried that mindset into business. Leadership isn't just about holding others accountable it's about being accountable yourself.

By setting clear expectations and leading by example, I created an environment where accountability was shared. Leaders must model the behavior they want to see in their teams, fostering a culture of trust, respect, and ownership. Accountability across generations not only bridges gaps but also inspires innovation and results. When everyone takes responsibility for their actions, it creates a more innovative and productive environment.

Final Thoughts:

Leadership isn't defined by age or experience, but by the ability to connect, inspire, and adapt. The generational divide in leadership is a challenge, but it's also an opportunity to build stronger, more cohesive teams. By focusing on principles like character, shared values, mentorship, and accountability, leaders can bridge any gap whether it's generational or otherwise.

Reflect on your leadership journey. What generational gaps do you face? How can you adjust your approach to foster collaboration and mutual respect? Are you leading by example and prioritizing accountability for yourself and your team?

Actionable Takeaways:

Lead with humility, not ego. Focus on the team's needs and embrace humility in decision-making.

Build a foundation of shared values. Make integrity, accountability, and respect the cornerstone of your leadership.

Mentor across generations. Embrace mentorship as a two-way street, learning from others while sharing your experience.

Emphasize accountability. Create a culture of mutual accountability by setting clear expectations and leading by example.

Make decisions with integrity. Stay true to your values and make decisions aligned with your core principles.

Closing the gap in leadership is about recognizing the strengths in others, respecting differences, and fostering an environment where everyone feels heard, valued, and empowered. Lead with purpose, integrity, and a commitment to building a lasting legacy.

About The Author

Earl Morrison is the founder of Leading and Learning with Character, L.L.C., a leadership development company focused on character-driven growth. With over 29 years of leadership experience, Earl brings a wealth of knowledge to help individuals and organizations overcome obstacles such as toxic work environments, poor communication, and lack of teamwork. As a retired Chief of Police and former Assistant Director, Earl understands the complexities of leadership and has firsthand experience in leading through adversity. He has helped numerous clients transform their organizations, improve their leadership practices, and create lasting change. Many clients often remark that they wish they had reached out sooner. Through his consulting, leadership training, and mentoring programs, Earl equips others with the strategies and skills they need to become effective leaders and propel their organizations forward.

www.earlmorrison.com

YouTube: LeadingWithCharacter2017 | Facebook: Earl Morrison Leading and Learning with Character | Instagram: Earl Morrison Leading | Linkedin: Earl Morrison | X: AndLeading

Chapter 9

B.R.E.A.T.H.E.: A Blueprint for Leading with Peace, Power, and Purpose
By: Dr. Obioma Martin

Have you ever found yourself gasping for air—not because you couldn't breathe physically, but because life's pressures made it feel impossible to keep going?

I remember the day I had to decide whether I was going to collapse under the weight of betrayal, loss, and broken promises—or rise and rebuild. My world had shifted overnight, and the life I thought I knew no longer existed. But in that moment, God whispered one word into my spirit: Breathe.

Not just the inhale and exhale that keeps us alive, but a sacred reminder to pause, center, and lean into His blueprint for my next season. That simple word became my compass, guiding me through valleys and mountain tops, teaching me how to lead my life and my business with integrity, resilience, and divine alignment.

This is how the B.R.E.A.T.H.E.™ Framework was born—not from theory, but from lived experience, forged in the fire of trials, and refined through years of leading women, building businesses, and serving communities around the world.

My Journey of Becoming

When I first stepped into entrepreneurship in 2001, I had no blueprint, no roadmap—only determination, faith, and the will to create something better for my children. What began as a side hustle grew into a licensed business. From there, I opened a daycare, launched a consulting company, built a nonprofit, and eventually established an ecosystem of enterprises—OMAX Institute, OmazingYou, OMART Women Supporting Women, and more.

For sixteen of those years, I was in business with my then-husband. We were partners in life and in business—until we were not. When the marriage ended, so did that partnership. The divorce was another crushing blow to my business and to my sense of stability. The separation nearly killed me emotionally, mentally, and financially. There were nights when the weight of grief and betrayal felt suffocating, and I wondered if I would ever rise again.

But in my darkest moment, I clung to a promise greater than my pain: "I can do all things through Christ who strengthens me" (Philippians 4:13). That Word became my lifeline. Slowly but surely, I began to rebuild— not just my business, but my spirit, my identity, and my vision. The end of that chapter in my personal life became the beginning of a new chapter in my leadership journey.

It was in those moments that B.R.E.A.T.H.E.™ shifted from survival to strategy—a spiritual and practical framework to lead not just myself, but thousands of others.

The B.R.E.A.T.H.E.™ Framework

B – Believe
Belief is the oxygen of leadership. Before anyone else could believe in me, I had to believe in myself. I had to trust that my vision was valid, even when the bank account said otherwise. Belief carried me when contracts were delayed, when staff walked out, and when critics questioned my credibility.

Takeaway: Leaders must first win the internal battle of belief before they can win external victories.

R – Release
Leadership requires release. I had to let go of toxic relationships, outdated business models, and the need to prove myself to people who would never clap for me. Releasing wasn't weakness—it was wisdom. Every release created room for new opportunities and aligned

partnerships to flow in.

Takeaway: What you release determines what you can receive.

E – Embrace
Embracing my authentic identity was one of the hardest yet most freeing steps. For years, I tried to fit into roles others designed for me: caretaker, employee, even "just another entrepreneur." But when I embraced that I was called to be a transformational leader, strategist, and voice for women, my businesses flourished.

Takeaway: Embrace your identity without apology. Authenticity is the currency of leadership.

A – Accept
Acceptance is about truth-telling. I had to accept what was in front of me—the numbers, the failures, the detours—without sugarcoating reality. Only then could I create solutions. Acceptance also meant receiving the grace of God daily, knowing that I am not perfect but always progressing.

Takeaway: Accept the truth, but don't let it limit your faith for the future.

T – Take Action
Dreams without action are fantasies. I learned to take bold, consistent action—launching programs, writing books, hosting retreats, and building teams—even when the timing didn't feel "perfect." Action silenced doubt and built momentum.

Takeaway: Clarity comes through action, not endless planning.

H – Heal
Healing was not optional; it was essential. I had to heal from rejection, disappointment, and the wounds of betrayal. Without healing, leaders bleed on the very people they are called to serve. My healing journey became the foundation for my coaching, retreats, and nonprofit work.

Takeaway: Unhealed leaders create unhealthy cultures. Heal first, then lead.

E – Elevate/Empower

The final step is elevation—not just for me, but for those I am called to empower. Leadership is not about climbing alone; it's about lifting others as you rise. From training women to earn credentials, to sponsoring housing for families, to mentoring global leaders, my mission is to empower others to breathe into their own destiny.

Takeaway: True leadership multiplies impact by elevating others.

Practical Lessons for Business & Life

From my journey and this framework, here are three actionable lessons every leader can apply:

1. Lead with Integrity. Do the right thing even when no one is watching. Integrity is the foundation of sustainable success.

2. Create Space for Renewal. Your best ideas and solutions won't come from burnout—they'll come from rest, prayer, and breathing space.

3. Build Legacy, Not Just Revenue. Money is important, but legacy outlives income. Every decision should align with the impact you want to leave behind.

Closing

As you read these words, I want to leave you with the same whisper that carried me through my darkest nights and my brightest days: Breathe.

Pause long enough to hear God's voice. Release what no longer serves you. Embrace your authentic calling. Accept the truth and still take bold action. Heal so you can lead with wholeness. Elevate and empower others as you rise.

Your life and leadership are not accidents they are divine assignments. The world is waiting for the sound of your breath, the strength of your voice, and the legacy only you can build.

So, my sister, my leader, my fellow world-changer, pause. Breathe. And step boldly into the leader you were always meant to be.

About The Author
Dr. Obioma Martin is an international speaker, business strategist, accountability coach, and 8x Amazon best-selling author. As CEO of OMAX Institute, OmazingYou, and founder of OMART Women Supporting Women, she empowers women to build sustainable businesses without sacrificing their souls. With two decades of global impact, her B.R.E.A.T.H.E.™ methodology has transformed thousands. A TEDx speaker and philanthropist, she equips leaders with tools to scale with clarity, courage, and confidence.

www.omazingyou.com
Facebook: Obioma Martin | Instagram: I Am Obioma Martin | YouTube: Obiomaorg

Chapter 10

The Unseen Advantage: Turning Silent Struggles into Purposeful Power
By: Coach Annie Pelissier

I remember sitting in yet another meeting where my ideas echoed off the walls but landed on no one. Surrounded by executives who didn't look like me, didn't think like me, and certainly didn't listen like me, I felt invisible. It wasn't the first time, and sadly, it wouldn't be the last. But what I didn't realize then was that being overlooked would become the very thing that ignited my mission.

For years, I played by the rules. I worked hard, kept my head down, and did everything they said would lead to success. Still, promotions passed me by, credit for my work was handed to others, and I became the go-to fixer without the recognition. I was praised in private and dismissed in public. It started to chip away at my confidence. But deep down, I knew I carried something powerful.

That "something" was my ability to see people. To advocate. To lead with compassion while still being strategic. What they ignored, I learned to nurture. When they left me out, I built my own room. That seed of pain grew into purpose. And that purpose birthed Elevate Consulting, a firm designed to help people rise, especially the ones the world tries to silence.

The hardest battle I faced wasn't in the boardroom. It was in my own mind. I had to unlearn the lie that I needed someone else to validate my worth. I had to rewrite the script that told me I was too much, too ambitious, too direct, too soft. I started listening to the quiet voice that said, "You are enough, and you have a calling."

Entrepreneurship didn't start with a business plan. It started with healing. I had to believe I was capable of more, even before I saw the evidence. I immersed myself in learning, coaching, and mindset work. I began to see that the things I once saw as flaws were my advantage.

No one tells you how taxing it is to build something from the ground up while still holding space for everyone else. As women, we are often the emotional, physical, and financial support systems for our families, teams, and communities. But who holds us up?

I learned that my body was the first business I needed to take care of. Burnout wasn't a badge of honor. I began to move with intention. I made rest a strategy, not a reward. I scheduled my wellness like I did my meetings. Because a woman on fire cannot sustain her impact if she's running on empty.

Your body is your business partner. Listen to it. Nourish it. Trust when it whispers before it has to scream.

The world tells women to hustle harder, but I learned to build smarter. Elevate Consulting wasn't born from desperation. It was born from divine alignment. I knew what it felt like to be the only Black woman in a room, to be expected to fix everything but not be invited to make the decisions. So, I built a business that makes room for others.

My company helps organizations attract, retain, and develop talent. But at the heart of it, we help people feel seen, valued, and supported. I also created the Elevate Me Blueprint, a coaching program to help women step into the roles they were always qualified for but too afraid to claim.

If you're reading this and wondering where to start, know this: You do not have to wait for someone to choose you. You can choose yourself. There will be seasons where you feel unseen, unheard, and uninvited. But that doesn't mean you don't belong. It means it's time to create the table, write the narrative, and lead in your own way. You are not behind. You are becoming.

Action Steps You Can Start Today:

1. Audit Your Inner Dialogue: Write down the top three limiting beliefs you catch yourself thinking during the week. Next to each, write a

new, empowering truth. Speak that new truth out loud daily for the next 30 days.

2. Protect Your Energy Like a Business Asset: Set a boundary this week. That could be saying no to a project, protecting a lunch break, or ending work at a set time. Put it on your calendar and honor it.

3. Identify Your Zone of Genius: Ask three people you trust, "What do you come to me for?" or "What do you think I'm great at that I might not see?" Look for patterns. This will help clarify your business sweet spot.

4. Build Brand with Heart: Craft one message that reflects the heart of your mission, why you do what you do and share it on your social media, email signature, or business card. People want to connect with your why.

5. Start Before You Feel Ready: Pick one action you've been putting off because you're waiting to feel 'ready' and do it this week. Send the email. Post the video. Launch the page. Imperfect action builds momentum.

6. Build Your Circle: Join a group, attend a virtual event, or send a message to someone you admire. Write down the names of five women who inspire you, then reach out to one. You don't need everyone, just a few who see you.

About The Author

Coach Annie is the powerhouse CEO and founder of Elevate Consulting, LLC, a leadership development and HR consulting firm devoted to helping professionals unlock their full potential and walk boldly in their purpose. With over 20 years of experience in human resources across corporate and nonprofit sectors, Annie brings a heart-centered yet strategic approach to leadership coaching, career advancement, and workplace transformation.

She is the bestselling author of *Taking Your Dreams Off Life Support*, a motivational guide that empowers professionals to break through fear, self-doubt, and stagnation. Her newest release, *kept in the Dark: Finding Faith When You Can't Feel God*, is a deeply personal 60-day devotional born from seasons of silence, struggle, and spiritual growth encouraging readers to trust even when the path isn't clear.

Through her signature coaching programs, Annie equips mid-level professionals, especially women with tools to build powerful personal brands, elevate their influence, and transition with confidence into senior leadership roles. Her work has helped clients secure major salary increases, navigate career pivots, and step into rooms they once felt unqualified to enter.

A passionate advocate for women in leadership, self-care, and purpose alignment, Annie uses her voice to inspire clarity, authenticity, and courage. She has delivered transformative talks for high schools, colleges, and corporate teams, always reminding her audience that where you start is never where you have to stay.

Firm in her belief that mindset, mentorship, and faith are the foundation for sustainable success, Annie is on a mission to help others rise not just in their careers, but in every area of life.

www.elevateconsultingsllc.com
Facebook & Instagram: CoachAnnie

Chapter 11

How To Rediscover Your Passion After Experiencing Trauma
By: Nicole D. Shepherd

Trauma has a way of silencing us. It robs us of the energy, creativity, and clarity we once had. Whether the trauma came from abuse, heartbreak, betrayal, loss, or unexpected life disruptions, it often leaves us feeling stuck, unsure of who we are and disconnected from he passions that once fueled us.

But here's the truth: trauma does not erase your purpose. Your passion is not gone; it is simply buried beneath layers of pain, fear, and self-protection. The journey of rediscovery begins when you dare to peel back those layers, reclaim your voice, and choose to step forward again.

Over the years, I developed a framework called **V.O.I.C.E.** that helps women reclaim their lives after trauma. Each letter represents a step in the healing journey: **Validate, Own, Identify, Cultivate, and Empower.** By walking through these stages, you can rediscover not just your passion but also the courage to live fully and authentically again.

V – Validate Your Experience

The first step to healing is validation. Too often, survivors of trauma minimize what they've been through. We say things like, "It wasn't that bad" or "Other people have it worse." But downplaying your pain doesn't erase it; it only buries it deeper.

Validation means acknowledging the reality of your trauma without shame or guilt. It means giving yourself permission to grieve, to feel angry, to be tired, to be human. Healing doesn't begin with pretending everything is fine. It begins with honesty.

When you validate your experience, you declare: *What I went through mattered. My pain is real. And I deserve to heal.*

Reflection Prompt: Write down what you experienced and allow yourself to name the emotions that still surface. Then affirm: *My story matters, and so do I.*

O – Own Your Story

After validating your experience, the next step is ownership. This doesn't mean taking responsibility for the harm someone else caused. It means reclaiming your narrative. Trauma may have been written into your story, but it does not get to be the final chapter.

Owning your story is an act of power. It's choosing to see yourself not as a victim, but as a survivor and eventually a thriver. When you take ownership, you shift from asking "Why did this happen to me?" to asking "How will I grow from this?"

Owning your story allows you to stand tall, unapologetically, in who you are. It invites you to share your truth, not for pity, but for freedom. Passion is often rediscovered when you dare to say out loud: *This is what I've been through, and this is who I'm becoming because of it.*

Reflection Prompt: Journal about a lesson your trauma taught you. How has it shaped your resilience, your empathy, or your sense of purpose?

I – Identify the Lies

Trauma often whispers lies that become embedded in our beliefs: "I'm not enough." "I'll never be happy again." "I don't deserve love." Left unchallenged, these lies become invisible chains that keep us from pursuing what sets our souls on fire.

Rediscovering your passion requires you to identify those lies and replace them with truth. Ask yourself: What beliefs am I carrying that do not serve me? Who told me this? And most importantly what does the truth say?

For me, the truth came from faith and scripture. But whether your anchor is spiritual, personal, or philosophical, grounding yourself in truth is essential. Because passion cannot grow in soil poisoned by lies.

Reflection Prompt: Write down the top three negative beliefs you carry. Next to each one, write a truth that sets you free. For example, replace "I'm broken" with "I am healing and whole."

C – Cultivate Boundaries and Confidence

When trauma shakes your life, it often leaves you vulnerable to unhealthy relationships, cycles of people-pleasing, or fear of setting limits. Rediscovering your passion requires creating a safe space for it to flourish—and that begins with cultivating boundaries.

Boundaries are not walls; they are fences with gates. They protect what's valuable while allowing in what nurtures you. By setting healthy boundaries, you signal to yourself and others: *My voice, my time, and my dreams are worthy of protection.*

Confidence also grows through small, consistent steps. The more you honor your boundaries and make choices aligned with your values, the more your confidence strengthens. With each step, your passion begins to resurface and not as a fleeting spark, but as a steady flame.

Reflection Prompt: Identify one boundary you need to set in your life. Write down how enforcing it will create space for your healing and passions to thrive.

E – Empower Others and Expand Your Purpose

The final step in the V.O.I.C.E. framework is empowerment. True healing becomes complete when you use your story to inspire others. Passion grows when it flows outward.

Empowerment doesn't always mean standing on a stage or writing a book. Sometimes it looks like encouraging a friend, mentoring someone who is where you once were, or creating art that carries hope. By sharing your journey, you remind others, yourself and that life after trauma is not only possible but powerful.

The greatest gift of rediscovering your passion is realizing it was never just for you. Your healing creates a ripple effect, expanding into your family, community, and beyond. When you empower others, you step fully into purpose.

Reflection Prompt: Consider one way you can share your story, gift, or passion with someone else this month. Write down the first action step to make it happen.

Bringing It All Together

Healing after trauma is not a straight path. There will be moments when you feel strong and moments when you feel like giving up. But the V.O.I.C.E. framework provides a roadmap back to yourself:

- **Validate** your experience and honor your pain.

- **Own** your story and shift from victim to survivor.

- **Identify** the lies and replace them with truth.

- **Cultivate** boundaries, confidence and protect your passion.

- **Empower** others and expand your purpose.

As you walk through these steps, passion will begin to reemerge. It may look different than before, but it will be deeper, stronger, and more aligned with your authentic self.

A Final Word of Hope

Trauma may have changed your story, but it does not define your destiny. Passion is not lost forever—it is waiting for you to rediscover it. You are not broken beyond repair. You are being rebuilt into someone more resilient, more compassionate, and more powerful than before.

When you reclaim your V.O.I.C.E., you don't just rediscover passion, you rediscover *you*.

About The Author

Pastor Nicole D. Shepherd is a dynamic global keynote speaker, visionary entrepreneur, and award-winning leader who empowers women to reclaim their voice and walk boldly in purpose. She is the founder of Jeri's Cheesecake Boutique, a thriving brand built on faith, creativity, and excellence, and the co-founder of Women Covering Women Empowerment Services, a platform dedicated to equipping women with tools for growth, resilience, and transformation.

As the creator of the V.O.I.C.E. Framework (Validate, Own, Identify, Cultivate, Empower), Nicole equips women to heal from trauma, rebuild their confidence, and lead authentically in life, business, and ministry. Her journey from Detroit to entrepreneurship is a testimony of resilience, grace, and God's transforming power. Whether on the mainstage, in the kitchen, or mentoring one-on-one, Nicole leads with passion, faith, and purpose. She proves that faith-led women can build, thrive, and make Kingdom impact across every arena.

Facebook & Instagram: NDS Coaching Services

Chapter 12

Rising Through Resilience: The Story Behind Anointed2Write
The Power of Voice and Visibility
Dr. Heather Robinson, Ph.D.

I never imagined that my greatest challenges would lead me to build a business that empowers others. Losing my mother at seven and my father at fifteen forced me to navigate the world differently. I had to become self-sufficient early, relying on my inner strength and determination. Life continued to test me losing two of my sisters back-to-back in 2021 and 2022 felt like a crushing blow. But through it all, I discovered my purpose: to give a voice to those who felt silenced.

Anointed2Write LLC was born from this realization. What started as a simple writing service evolved into a platform that amplifies voices, champions diversity, and fosters transformation. I knew that storytelling was powerful, but I soon realized that empowerment and education were equally important. People needed more than just a book they needed strategy, visibility, and guidance to create real impact.

Growing up, I always had an innate desire to teach, mentor, and uplift others. My academic journey reinforced that passion. I obtained my Bachelor's degree in African-American Studies from Temple University, followed by a Master's in Early Childhood Education from Grand Canyon University. I later pursued 15 Post-Graduate credits in Education from Gwynedd Mercy University and earned my Ph.D. in Education Leadership and Diverse Ministry Education from Heart Bible International University.

My degrees and life experiences taught me that education was not just about learning it was about liberation. Education had given me the tools to navigate the world with confidence, and I wanted to provide that same empowerment to others. That's what led me to create Anointed2Write LLC, a business built on the foundation of storytelling, equity, and transformation.

The Journey of Anointed2Write: From Vision to Movement

When I first launched Anointed2Write, my goal was to help people tell their stories. I saw the gaps—so many individuals had powerful experiences and wisdom to share but lacked the resources, confidence, or platform to bring them to life. I wanted to change that.

However, the more I worked with clients, the more I saw the bigger picture. It wasn't just about writing—it was about helping people stand in their power. This realization pushed me to pivot. I began integrating my expertise in education and DEI (Diversity, Equity, and Inclusion) into my business, ensuring that Anointed2Write was not just a publishing company but a vehicle for transformation.

One pivotal moment that solidified my mission was realizing the misconceptions surrounding DEI. Many people still think DEI is just a "Black thing." That blew my mind. DEI is about everyone. It's about breaking down barriers, fostering inclusivity, and ensuring that every voice has a seat at the table. Once people truly understand that, real change can happen.

That's what Anointed2Write represents—bridging the gaps that separate us and creating spaces where everyone can thrive.

Lessons and Strategies for Success
Visibility and Credibility Go Hand in Hand
One of my guiding principles is: Credibility + Visibility = Equitability.

Many entrepreneurs and thought leaders have the expertise, but they remain unseen. If people don't know your work exists, how can you create an impact? Visibility is essential, but it must be backed by credibility. That's why I focus on helping individuals and organizations elevate their platforms while ensuring their message is clear, authoritative, and valuable.

Actionable Takeaway: Find ways to increase your visibility while maintaining credibility. Speak at events, publish content, engage in discussions, and align yourself with reputable organizations. Your presence should match your expertise.

Pivoting Is Not Failing—It's Expanding
Many entrepreneurs hesitate to pivot because they see it as abandoning their original vision. I see it differently. Pivoting allowed me to expand my mission, impact, and reach.

Initially, Anointed2Write was about storytelling. But as I evolved, I realized I could do more by integrating DEI consulting, educational training, and strategic branding. This shift didn't erase my original vision—it enhanced it.

Actionable Takeaway: Be willing to adjust your approach as you grow. The market, your clients, and your expertise will evolve—allow your business to do the same.

Your Story Is Your Power
One of the biggest mistakes entrepreneurs make is underestimating the power of their own journey. People don't just buy products or services—they invest in people, missions, and movements. Sharing my personal journey—my losses, struggles, and victories—has been one of the most powerful tools in growing my business and building authentic connections.

Actionable Takeaway: Embrace your story. Use it to connect with your audience, establish credibility, and inspire others to take action.

Making an Impact Through Education and Empowerment

One of my biggest projects to date is the Educators Rise: Voices of Change Anthology, Volume 1—a collection of stories from educators sharing challenges, triumphs, and transformative strategies in education. This book is more than just pages bound together—it's a movement that fosters understanding, sparks dialogue, and promotes actionable change.

Beyond the anthology, I'm also hosting the Educators Rise Conference and Awards Gala, where influential voices in education and DEI will come together to share insights, strategies, and inspiration. Attendees will earn CPD credits, furthering their professional growth while engaging in powerful conversations.

As a certified CPD Consultant, I am actively pitching myself for speaking engagements and training sessions. Why? Because knowledge isn't enough—we need action. DEI isn't just about awareness; it's about implementation, strategy, and lasting change.

Advice for Women Entrepreneurs

To any woman reading this who is dreaming of starting her own venture, here's what I want you to know:

Your voice matters. Don't let fear keep you silent.
Start before you feel ready. There is no perfect time—just take the leap.

Stay authentic. People resonate with realness. Don't try to fit into a mold.

Use your story as fuel. Your experiences are not obstacles—they are stepping stones.

Balancing entrepreneurship with personal well-being is challenging, but it's possible. I prioritize self-care by finding small moments—whether it's a quick coffee break or a quiet 15-minute shower. Every role I take on as an educator, advocate, consultant, and business leader is part of my larger mission. And staying aligned with that mission keeps me grounded.

Closing Reflections: The Future of Anointed2Write

Anointed2Write has grown beyond what I originally imagined, but I know this is just the beginning. My next goal is to take Educators Rise: Voices of Change into universities, sparking meaningful conversations and inspiring change on a larger scale. I am also preparing for Volume 2 of the anthology, expanding the voices and perspectives that need to be heard.

If there's one thing I want you to take away from this, it's this: Your journey has value. Your voice has power. And your impact is waiting to be made.

Whatever your passion, your expertise, or your calling step into it boldly. The world needs your voice, your vision, and your unique brilliance. Don't wait. Start now. Rise.

About The Author

A dedicated wife to Elder Christopher Robinson, Dr. Heather A. Robinson is a renowned leader in education advocacy and DEI consulting. As the founder of Anointed2Write LLC in Exton, PA, Heather empowers individuals and organizations through education, visibility, and advocacy. She holds a Bachelor's in African-American Studies from Temple University, a Master's in Early Childhood Education from Grand Canyon University, and a Ph.D. in Organizational Educational Leadership from Heart Bible International University. With over 20 years of experience, Heather has received the Presidential Lifetime Achievement Award, three global awards, Inspiring Women's Educators Award, and Educator of the Year.

A prolific author and dynamic speaker, she has been on nine stages, featured in numerous magazines and podcasts. Heather's company offers services for aspiring authors, speakers, and organizations, including writing and public speaking programs, anthology curation assistance, and education consultant services. As an Education Advocate

& DEI consultant, she helps organizations create inclusive cultures through professional development, equity audits, and consulting. Heather's mantra, "Visibility + Credibility = Equitability," reflects her commitment to fostering equity and inclusion.

www.Anointed2Write.com
Instagram: Anointed2Write | Facebook: Anointed2WriteLLC | Linkedin: Dr Heather Robinson

Chapter 13

No Perfect Timing, Just Perfect Faith
By: Erica Jefferson

My name is Erica Jefferson, and I'm a licensed esthetician and the proud owner of Snatching Bodies Beauti Bar in Hampton, Virginia. I specialize in sugaring, waxing, vajacials, facials, and back-and-butt facials. Truth be told, my work goes far beyond skincare and smooth results. What I really do is help women feel confident in their own skin, reclaim their softness, and prioritize themselves in a world that constantly tells them to put everything and everyone else first.

Let me keep it real, I didn't start here before I went all in on myself, I was working a full-time 9 to 5 job and picking up hours as a part-time esthetician. On paper, my life looked stable. I had the "good job" with benefits, the steady paycheck, the routine. But in reality? I was exhausted. I was over it. Day after day, I clocked into something that didn't light me up, while my dream sat on the back burner. What finally opened my eyes was the numbers. One day, I realized my part-time income as an esthetician was actually surpassing what I made working full-time. That was my wake-up call. It didn't make sense to give 40 hours a week to something I didn't love when my passion was already proving it could sustain me.

So, I made the decision to transition out of the nine-to-five grind and go full-time in my business and just as I took that leap, COVID hit.

Talk about timing. Just when I decided to leave the safety of my full-time job and step into entrepreneurship full-time, the world shut down. Businesses closed. People were scared. The uncertainty was heavy. And here I was, betting it all on myself. To some people, it looked reckless. To me, it was necessary. The truth is, if you're waiting for the "perfect time," you'll be waiting forever. There will always be something in the way either bills, fear, a shaky economy, or too much competition. If you're waiting for every light to turn green before you move, you'll be stuck at the intersection for life.

So, I moved anyway. While the doors of my beauty bar were closed, I went to work behind the scenes. I built my brand. I invested in marketing education. I built systems so I'd be ready when the world opened again, and I stayed visible. Even though I couldn't service clients in person, I made sure they still saw me online sharing tips, educating, showing up consistently. That consistency made all the difference. When restrictions were lifted and people were ready to book again, I wasn't starting at zero. My name was already in their minds.

For me, this was never just about hair removal or facials. This was about transformation. I've always believed that confidence is a game-changer. When a woman feels good about herself, her whole energy shifts. She walks taller. She speaks with authority. She goes after what she wants with a fire that can't be ignored. And when she doesn't? She shrinks. She second-guesses. She hesitates. I wanted to be part of shifting that energy. I wanted to create a space where women especially women who look like me could feel cared for, seen, and affirmed. It's not just what pushed me to start it's what continues to fuel me today.

Opening during COVID was one of the hardest things I've ever done, but truthfully, entrepreneurship is hard, pandemic or not. Some struggles don't get glamorized on Instagram but are very real:

1. Isolation. People don't always understand your grind. Friends and family may question why you left the "secure" job. Entrepreneurship can feel lonely.

2. Money pressure. Early on, what's coming in doesn't always match what's going out. Bills don't stop just because business is slow. It's a constant tug-of-war between faith and fear.

3. Imposter syndrome. You'll look at others in your industry and wonder if you're really cut out for this. That voice doesn't disappear overnight.

4. Client inconsistency. One week you're fully booked, the next you're staring at empty slots. The rollercoaster is real.

These are the pain points that can either break you or build you. For me, I decided to let them build me.
At first, these lessons helped me survive the startup phase. Over time, I realized they aren't just for getting started they're the principles that continue to sustain me today.

1. Lead With Your Why.
Your why is your anchor. It's what gets me out of bed when I'm tired, and it's the reason my clients connect with me beyond the service. People don't just buy what you do—they buy into why you do it.

2. Stop Waiting for Perfect.
If I had waited for the "right time," I'd still be stuck at that nine-to-five. Perfection doesn't exist. Progress does. Done will always be better than perfect.

3. Stay Visible.
Visibility isn't just for starting—it's for sustaining. I show up even when I'm busy, because consistency builds trust. Clients need to know you're still here, still showing up, still invested.

4. Build a Community.
Clients come for the service, but they stay for the experience. My goal has always been to create a safe, affirming space. That sense of community is what gives a business longevity.

5. Pivot When Needed.
COVID forced me to pivot quickly, but that lesson still applies. Flexibility keeps me growing. Whether it's adjusting services, pricing, or marketing, I've learned not to be afraid of change.

6. Invest in Yourself.
The money I put into education, mentorship, and systems didn't just help me get off the ground—it continues to pay me today. Growth comes when you stop viewing everything as an expense and start treating it as an investment.

7. Protect Your Mindset.
This is the hardest part. Fear and doubt don't magically go away when you leave your nine-to-five. They still show up. The difference is, I've learned how to fight back. Protecting my mental space and surrounding myself with supportive people is non-negotiable.

Looking back, I'm grateful I didn't let fear or even a global pandemic stops me. What started as a part-time hustle while I dragged myself through a draining 9 to 5 has grown into a full-time business that changes lives. Today, Snatching Bodies Beauti Bar is more than a beauty bar. It's a community. It's transformation. And its proof that your passion can outgrow your paycheck if you let it. What looked like the worst timing became my greatest teacher.

COVID forced me to be intentional, resourceful, and resilient. And those same lessons keep me grounded today. Now, I don't just serve clients. I mentor other beauty professionals who are ready to bet on themselves and build something of their own because if I could do it during one of the hardest times in history, I know others can too.

If you're waiting for a sign, this is it. You're reading these words for a reason. I know what it feels like to be tired of playing small, to feel the weight of potential that's never fully unleashed. I also know the freedom of saying "yes" to yourself even when it's scary, even when it doesn't make sense. Don't wait for another year, another month, another day. Your time is now.

About The Author

Erica Jefferson is a licensed esthetician, entrepreneur, and founder of Snatching Bodies Beauti Bar in Hampton, Virginia. After leaving her nine-to-five to pursue her passion full-time during the height of the COVID-19 pandemic, she transformed a part-time hustle into a thriving luxury spa brand.

Her journey of starting during one of the hardest seasons for small businesses taught her lessons in resilience, visibility, and consistency that she now shares with others. As she continues to expand her brand, Erica is stepping into mentoring and educating other beauty professionals, helping them build profitable, purpose-driven businesses rooted in confidence and clarity.

Passionate about women prioritizing themselves and walking in their power, Erica uses her story to inspire others to stop waiting for the "perfect time" and start anyway.

www.snatchingbodiesbeautibar.com
Facebook: Erica Jefferson

Chapter 14

From Paralysis to Power: Transforming Trauma into Business Success
By: Toni Chavis

The morning I woke up paralyzed from the neck down marked a turning point in my military career, just eighteen months' shy of retirement eligibility. This wasn't a sudden occurrence – it was the culmination of a two-year battle with my own body. What started as restless leg syndrome evolved into an all-consuming constellation of symptoms: debilitating pain, numbness, and hypersensitivity that touched every aspect of my life. As a military training instructor, I pushed through exhaustion, working overtime to compensate for my declining focus, determined to fulfill my duties despite my deteriorating health.

The medical system's response was a carousel of appointments and prescriptions – twenty-seven different medications at its peak, ultimately leading to a Fibromyalgia diagnosis, a label that seemed more like a surrender than a solution. When that diagnosis triggered a non-deployable status, the military machinery began moving to process my medical discharge. That paralytic morning, with my husband helping me sit upright, I made a silent vow: this would not be my ending. What followed was an eighteen-month battle through paperwork, medical boards, and bureaucratic hurdles, all while wrestling with the betrayal of an institution I'd faithfully served.

Though I secured my medical retirement with full benefits, the victory felt hollow. The medical community's verdict was clear: my working days were over. For two years, my sofa became my prison as depression wrapped its heavy chains around me. Three autoimmune diseases threatened to become my new identity. But in those darkest moments, a familiar voice emerged – the same voice that had guided a terrified five-year-old through domestic violence, that had strengthened a single mother through countless struggles, that had carried me through the devastating loss of a child at seven months' gestation.

That voice whispered one powerful word: "Rise.

"This pivotal moment became the catalyst for "Courageous Women Rise Up" (CWRU), an organization born from my personal transformation journey. Our mission resonates deeply: "Transforming how high-achieving women navigate stress and trauma, creating sustainable success through holistic practices that honor both professional excellence and personal power." This isn't just a mission statement – it's a revolution in how women approach healing while building their empires.

Stress Response Management: The Foundation of Recovery when trauma lives in your body, every business challenge can trigger a cascade of physical responses. I learned this firsthand during my recovery, where managing stress became as crucial as any business strategy.

Through deliberate practice, I developed a system to recognize stress triggers before they escalated into physical symptoms. This meant creating daily routines that honored my body's signals and implementing recovery protocols after triggering events.

Professional Boundary Intelligence: The Power of Protected Space.

One of the most challenging lessons I learned was that success without boundaries is merely exhaustion wearing a crown. As someone who witnessed domestic violence and navigated toxic relationships, I had to relearn what healthy boundaries looked like in a professional context. This meant:

- Developing the courage to say "no" without guilt
- Creating clear communication protocols for client expectations
- Establishing work-life integration that honored my healing journey
- Breaking free from people-pleasing patterns that stemmed from trauma

Emotional Resilience: From Survival Mode to Strategic Growth.

Emotional resilience isn't about being unbreakable – it's about becoming unshakeable. My journey from domestic violence survivor to military veteran to successful business owner taught me that true resilience grows from acknowledging our wounds while refusing to be defined by them. This resilience became the cornerstone of my business success, enabling me to:

- Build support systems that understand both trauma history and business goals
- Develop problem-solving skills that account for emotional triggers
- Create recovery strategies that honor both past and future

Mindset Transformation: Rewriting Your Story.

The shift from trauma survivor to business leader required a complete mindset overhaul. I had to challenge the perfectionism that had protected me during trauma but now hindered my growth. This transformation involved:

- Replacing negative self-talk with empowering narratives
- Moving from perfectionism to progress-focused thinking
- Developing self-compassion as a business strategy
- Learning to celebrate achievements without diminishment

Holistic Well-being Integration: The Missing Link in Business Success.

The path from trauma to triumph requires more than traditional business strategies – it demands a holistic approach to well-being. When I started my home improvement business and pursued my Master of Fine Arts in Interior Design, I realized that sustainable success meant integrating healing practices into every aspect of my work life.

This integration includes:

- Implementing consistent self-care practices that support business growth
- Developing sustainable wellness habits that enhance professional performance
- Creating boundaries that protect both your healing journey and your business goals

Remember, self-love and self-care aren't selfish – they're essential investments in your business
success. Every woman carrying trauma while building a business needs to understand this fundamental truth: Your healing journey isn't separate from your business journey – it's an integral part of your success story.

As someone who has transformed from a paralyzed veteran into a thriving business owner, I can tell you that your trauma doesn't have to be your business liability. When properly processed and integrated, it becomes your unique advantage – fueling your determination, deepening your empathy, and strengthening your resilience.

The journey from paralysis to power isn't linear. It's a daily commitment to growth, healing, and transformation. But with the right tools, support, and mindset, every woman can rise from her challenges to create not just a successful business, but a life that honors both her struggles and her strength.

Your Journey Begins Now: If my story resonates with you, if you've found yourself nodding along, knowing deep down that you're capable of more but feeling trapped by past trauma or current circumstances, you're not alone. Every day, I meet brilliant, high-achieving women who are:

- Juggling multiple responsibilities while pursuing ambitious goals
- Carrying the weight of past trauma or significant life challenges

About The Author

Hello, I'm Toni Chavis, the CEO of TTC Enterprises ~ Opulent Designs, and my life is a testament to resilience. From a home improvement specialist and interior design graduate to a business coach, realtor, mentor, and author, my journey is one of overcoming and empowerment. My books, including "A Diamond Born of Fortitude," "Rise Above," "One DAE at a Time," and "Take the Muzzle Off," reflect my narrative. My path took an unexpected detour as my military career was nearing its end when I woke up one morning, paralyzed from the neck down due to stress-induced health issues. Despite the medical community's grim prognosis, my indomitable spirit prevailed.

I was motivated by the needs of others and embarked on a mission to regain my strength, focus, faith, and family connections. Facing three autoimmune diseases and environmental health challenges, I minimized my medication use and harnessed the power of a positive mindset and natural healing. This resilience fueled me to start a thriving home improvement business with my husband and achieve a Master of Fine Arts in Interior Design. Now, I am a sought-after motivational speaker, using my story to inspire changes in health, personal development, and community leadership.

I proudly serve my community in the Hampton Roads area of Virginia, as a board member of several organizations, and made history as the first African American female President of the York County Chamber of Commerce in 2020 - 2022.

With a background in Telecommunications Management and Education and Training Management, and a Bachelor of Science from Southern Illinois University in Adult Workforce Education and Development, I bridge gaps between military and civilian sectors to help them communicate more effectively. My life's roles as a mother, wife, MiMi, designer, and veteran are driven by my experiences with Lupus, Fibromyalgia, domestic violence advocacy, and military trauma. "I am committed to empowering women to fully realize their potential in both personal and professional realms. My goal is to help them navigate and improve their mental and physical health by addressing chronic conditions caused by stress and past traumas. I strive to help them reclaim their self-confidence and cultivate resilience. My role is to uplift and inspire, demonstrating that despite any challenges, it is possible to rise above and thrive."

www.courageouswomanriseup.com
Instagram: Courageous Woman Rise Up – T Chavis | Tiktok: Courageous Woman1

Chapter 15

Your $100K Year and Why It's Closer Than You Think

By: Nicholas Marque

I Did It... Wait, I Did It?

I did it.
I did it!
I did it...?

$129,880.16. That's what my bookkeeper sent me, and I had to double-check it.

I had officially passed the $100,000 mark in revenue—and didn't even realize it. No champagne. No confetti. Just a regular Tuesday, and a realization that something had finally clicked.

This chapter isn't about hustle and grind. It's about what really gets you paid: clarity, focus, and strategy. If you've been stuck in "do more" mode, let this be your official invitation to shift gears.

Before the Money: The Bonus and the Breakdown

Let me take you back.

Before I was the *"Launching King,"* I was deep in the event industry—running my own event business and managing events full-time at a corporate job. I even upsold one of our contracts to nearly a million dollars.

You'd think that kind of success would come with job security, right?

Not exactly.

Weeks after delivering my best numbers yet, the pandemic hit. I was laid off. And my event clients? Gone. Canceled. Ghosted.

So I did what any multi-passionate entrepreneur might do I tried everything.

I launched a cookbook.
Started a YouTube cooking show.
Considered investing in an ATM vending machine.
Even wrote a TV show.

Entrepreneurial brains are wild, aren't they?

But amidst all that chaos, something powerful happened: people kept asking me to help them start their businesses. That was the goldmine I hadn't seen coming.

You're Closer Than You Think—If You Focus

The biggest turning point in my business?

I stopped trying to be all things to all people.
I got clear on what I wanted to be known for.
And I built everything around launching businesses.

I didn't just want clients—I wanted impact. I didn't want to get paid—I wanted to get paid well for doing what I do best.

Once I focused, the six-figure year didn't just happen—it became inevitable.

Shift #1: From Scrambling to Premium

In 2020, I was offering it all.

Virtual assistant staffing.
 Social media management.
Admin services.
Marketing and project management.

I was doing the most for the least.

Managing overseas contractors, juggling multiple client relationships, and working on tasks that didn't even light me up left me drained. I made $10,000 to $15,000 in a few months, but it didn't feel sustainable.

So I made my first real shift: I simplified and raised my prices.

I moved to a premium offer suite, focused on consulting, brand strategy, and launch services for serious entrepreneurs.

When you price with confidence, you attract commitment—not complaints.

Shift #2: It's not hocus pocus—It's FOCUS

In 2021, I doubled down on focus.

I narrowed in on just one to two high-ticket offers and brought in $65,000. Not bad. But in 2022, with just two clients, I brought in over $72,000.

The secret?

I wasn't doing more. I was doing the right things.

I turned unused trainings into digital products and upsells—without creating anything new from scratch.

Signature program? Check.
Coaching and courses? Packaged.
Income? Predictable.

Shift #3: Build a Team That Thinks, Not Just Tasks

I built my business with just me and a VA. But as I grew, I needed more than task-doers. I needed strategists—people who could think, make decisions, and drive results in their zone of genius.

I stopped managing everything myself and started hiring people who could run with the vision.

We now market one signature program with intention. From Passion to Profit is my flagship offer—but more importantly, I am known as the guy to go to when you want to launch a business.

That positioning is what drives our consulting clients, strategic partnerships, and even our event opportunities.

You can't grow what you don't measure—and you can't measure what you don't track.

Real Clients. Real Focus. Real Money.

One of my clients came in doing the most. She was a family lawyer... but also doing real estate closings, personal injury, and running a dropshipping store.

I mean, I'd expect nothing less from an entrepreneur.

We helped her focus on one niche: father's rights. We branded her, systematized her client journey, and positioned her as the go-to expert in that space.

Today, she generates over $50,000 a month in revenue, books 60 to 70 qualified leads monthly, and is opening her second office.

Another client was a chef selling "custom cuisine" door to door. If you could pronounce it, she'd cook it.

We helped her brand around what she was already known for: upscale soul food. That clarity helped her launch a food truck, then a restaurant, and now she's running a thriving multi–six-figure business.

These results weren't from throwing spaghetti at the wall. They were from focused, strategic business development—and the exact frameworks I used to reach my first six figures.

What I Want You to Take Away

You don't need to be on every platform.
You don't need to sell everything under the sun.
You don't need a hundred clients.

What you do need is a clear message, a focused offer, a trackable plan, and a system that works even when you're not working.

It's easier to charge a premium than it is to charge pennies.

And trust me—making more with less hustle? That's the part nobody tells you about until you're on the other side of six figures.

Whether you're launching your first business, trying to cross the $100K mark, or ready to add another six figures to your bottom line, let this chapter be your proof:

It's possible. It's practical. And it's a lot closer than you think.

Free Resource: Watch the $100K Training

Want to see exactly how I mapped out my six-figure business?
Access my private training originally shared with my high-level clients:

Watch the training: www.nicholasmarque/6figurejourney

Inside, I walk through the numbers, the strategy, and the mindset shifts that made it possible so you can use the same roadmap in your own journey.

About The Author

Nicholas Marque, known as Coach Nick, is an award-winning business coach and strategist recognized by NY Weekly as one of the Top 10 Business Coaches to Watch. As founder of CEO Mentality LLC, he helps small business owners transform their ideas into thriving six- and seven-figure companies. Nicholas is known for his dynamic, practical approach to sales, marketing, operations, and leadership—equipping entrepreneurs with clear strategies they can implement immediately. His powerful keynotes and workshops inspire audiences to think bigger, execute with confidence, and scale strategically. With a mission to help entrepreneurs stop playing small and build businesses that create lasting impact, Nicholas delivers the tools, insights, and motivation needed to turn vision into profit.

www.nicholasmarque.com
Instagram| Facebook| YouTube| LinkedIn: Nicholas Marque

Chapter 16

From Combat Boots to CEO in Power Suits:

How I Traded Permission for Purpose, Reclaimed My Voice, and Built
the Empire I Was Born to Lead.

By: Rosie Thames

> *"Your story is someone else's survival guide. Don't die with it inside you."*
> — Coach Rosie Thames

> *"They triumphed over him by the blood of the Lamb and by the word of their testimony."*
> — Revelation 12:11 (NIV)

I never set out to be a coach, a speaker, or a bestselling author. I simply said yes to one opportunity: joining an anthology called *Lift Launch Lead*. That one, yes, became my defining moment. Writing my first chapter transformed me. The confidence I gained, the visibility I received, and the lives I impacted lit a fire in me that couldn't be extinguished. Before I knew it, people were asking, "How did you do it? How can I write my story too?" That, sis, was the moment I realized I wasn't just called to share my story—I was called to help others unleash theirs.

Long before the world knew me as Coach Rosie, I proudly wore a different uniform. I served 20 years in the U.S. Air Force, enlisting in 2001 and retiring in 2021. Yet, even in uniform, I was unknowingly being shaped as an entrepreneur. I dipped into network marketing in 2005 and went on to build a six-figure empire with my then business partner. Together, we made history as the first Black and military couple to rise to the top ranks of the company. It wasn't a pivot to entrepreneurship— it was an evolution. That season of leadership shaped me as a builder, a mentor, and a woman who could confidently lead at scale—skills I now carry into my own brand.

But launching Coach Rosie Empire was a different game. In network marketing, I led a team of thousands, but when I stepped out to build my own brand, I had to lead myself. The transition wasn't seamless. There was imposter syndrome, uncertainty, and a whole lot of messy middle. I had to remind myself: just because it's new doesn't mean it's not valuable.

One pivotal moment that reshaped how I do business came from the tension between duty and devotion. In the military, your time isn't your own. I missed moments with my children and had to ask permission to care for my family. I carried guilt for choosing my loved ones over my obligations. That mindset stayed with me even after I retired—until I realized I no longer needed permission. Now, I run a business that gives me time freedom, family freedom, and the flexibility to lead with faith. I don't ask. I decide. I'm the CEO of my life. That's the true power of ownership.

Building a business came with a roller coaster of emotions. Starting was exciting but also terrifying. At times I questioned if I was qualified, worthy, or even capable. But I leaped. I built anyway. And what I discovered along the way was this: my story my ups, downs, trials, and triumphs wasn't just for me. It was a survival guide for someone else.

That truth became the heartbeat of my business. I started helping other women unmute their voices, share their stories, and turn pain into purpose. I saw firsthand how storytelling could heal, empower, and build a platform for profit. Many of my clients had been silenced for years by trauma or tradition. Through the work we did together, they began to say boldly, "Here I am. This is my truth."

But let's be real the beginning wasn't glamorous. I constantly compared myself to other entrepreneurs. I looked at their polished brands and thought, "Why doesn't mine look like that?" What I had to realize is that entrepreneurship is like a construction zone. In the early stages, it's all cones, dust, and chaos. The vision God gave me was beautiful, but the building process? Not so much. Still, I had to trust the process and the One who designed it.

I've learned from mentors that it's not enough to tell a story it has to mean something. But what truly transformed my business is this core truth: your story is someone else's survival guide. I teach my clients that their lived experiences are their greatest credentials. You don't need a degree to become a coach, speaker, or consultant you need clarity, courage, and the confidence to say, "I've lived through this, and now I'm going to lead through it.

So how do you begin? First, just start. Perfection is a trap. Done is better than perfect. Second, get help. Invest in coaches and mentors. Find your community. And third, trust the process even when it feels slow, silent, or stuck. Growth is happening even when you can't see it.

This approach helped my clients shift from fear to freedom. Many of them used voice-to-text tools to get their messy first drafts out. We celebrated progress over perfection. The result? Books were written. Stories were shared. Bestsellers were born.

One myth I constantly bust is that you have to be a "writer" to become an author. Not true. All you need is a story and the willingness to share it. You also don't need a fancy publisher. Anthologies like *Biz Her Way* are powerful, profitable, and a smart way to gain visibility. In fact, my first anthology chapter turned a $3,500 investment into over $55,000 in revenue in just 60 days. That's when I realized that stories don't just inspire they sell.

Of course, I made mistakes. I undercharged. I gave away my genius. I let clients slide on payments. But I learned quickly that I had to charge my worth, protect my time, and create systems that support sustainable growth. I now use third-party platforms that allow clients to pay in installments while I get paid up front. That's how you protect your brilliance.

The mindset that took me from stuck to successful? Asking for help. Modeling success. Delegating. And giving myself grace. I stopped trying to do everything myself and started investing in coaches, teams, and systems. I don't have to prove I can do it all. I just have to do what I'm called to do and do it well.

Today, my definition of success has evolved. It's not just about goals or income. It's about impact. It's about gratitude. It's about looking back and realizing: I didn't give up. I've fallen. I've been bruised. But I've risen. And every scar tells a story.

So what makes my journey uniquely mine? Everything. From growing up in Jamaica, to deploying to Iraq, to raising a son with special needs while running an empire, my journey is flavored with faith, fire, and resilience. My fingerprint is on every client I serve. I've built my brand from my battles, and that's what makes it unstoppable. I bring all of that to my brand. My clients don't just get a coach, they get a comeback queen who's lived what she teaches.

To the woman who's afraid to leap? Sis jump. Or let someone push you. I once had to jump off a platform in Japan onto a giant net while ziplining. I froze. I told the guide to push me. And he did. Sometimes you don't need more time. You need more courage or someone who will push you into your next level.

After reading this chapter, I want you to believe again. In your story. In your voice. In the power of your next move. Your time is now. Don't do it alone. Get the help. Find your community. Start messy. Start scared. But start because someone's waiting for your survival guide.

Quote to Remember: *Your story is someone else's survival guide.*

About the Author

Rosie Thames, also known as Coach Rosie, is a retired U.S. Air Force veteran turned bestselling author, award-winning speaker, and elite book coach. As the founder of Coach Rosie Empire, she empowers high-achieving women to unmute their voices, write powerful stories, and build profitable platforms with purpose. A proud Jamaican-born leader, Rosie blends faith, fire, and fearless storytelling to help others turn their mess into a message and their story into a legacy.

Facebook: Rosie Thames

Chapter 17

The $20K Wake-Up Call: Reclaiming My Voice, My Brand, My Purpose
By: Barbara J. Beckley

What if I told you that in three years, I spent over $20,000 building someone else's dream, while quietly burying my own? That I showed up, smiled, served, and supported with excellence, only to realize my mission had taken a backseat. I joined a business community with hopes of visibility and growth, and I got that—but not in the way I expected. I became the background singer in someone else's lead song.

The Seduction of Visibility
I still remember the excitement of joining that network. It was full of inspiring, like-minded professionals, all chasing success and service. I had access to incredible rooms, stages, and conversations. I was being seen. I was being heard. Or so I thought.

I was frequently asked to host events, lead small groups, and even help plan major summits. On the surface, it looked like I had "arrived." But in those three years, I never once led with my brand name. I was known for supporting *their* events, never for launching my own.

I mistook exposure for expansion. I was visible but not *rooted.* I was present but not *planted.*

The Cost of Disconnection
After three years of service, I felt something deep in my spirit. I was working harder for someone else's dream than I was for myself. So, I did something I had never done before—an audit.
I reviewed every receipt, every membership fee, travel expense, branding investment, tech tool, donation, and offering I had given during that time. When I added it all up, the number stared back at me: $20,000. Not invested in *my* brand. Not in *my* purpose. Not into *my* voice.
I discovered I had paid for branding materials for a community initiative, but hadn't updated my website in over two years. I sponsored

giveaways and raffles but hadn't invested in coaching or advertising for my services. My light was being
used to shine on someone else's stage.

From Breakdown to Breakthrough
When the reality hit, I was angry. But even more than that, I was heartbroken. How did I let this happen? And then, the breakthrough came: this wasn't a loss—it was a lesson.
I always ask myself: What is the *bigger picture*? This was my wake-up call.

Here are the 4 lessons that turned my $20K mistake into a foundation for greatness:

1. *Resilience is Built in the Valley*
    That moment of realization broke me, but it also shaped me. I learned that resilience isn't about bouncing back—it's about building better.

I started a journal that day called "The Rebuild." In it, I mapped out what I would do differently. Within six months, I launched my own branded show, and I brought on my *first* paying client as a visibility coach.

2. *You Need a Plan to Protect Your Purpose*
    I had been moving without a blueprint. I didn't have a plan that safeguarded my time, money, or mission.

I created a simple one-page business plan that included boundaries: what I would say yes to, what aligned with my brand, and how much time I would give to external projects.

3. *Coaching is Not Optional*
    I realized that I needed guidance. The right coach can help you see your blind spots and protect your progress.

I hired a business coach, and within three sessions, we uncovered a gap in my offers. I built out a package that started bringing consistent income instead of one-off projects.

4. *Never Give Your Voice Away to Someone Else's Platform*
   You can support others, but never at the cost of silencing yourself.

I rebranded my speaking engagements and began introducing myself as "CEO of Diamond Factor Network" every single time—even when on someone else's stage. It was no longer about being a guest, but about showing up with purpose and presence.

You may not be able to get the money back. I know I didn't. But you can reclaim your message. You can rebuild your momentum. You can rise again—wiser, bolder, more aligned.
Ask yourself: What are you investing in? Is your time, energy, and money building *your* vision?

Action Steps & Takeaways
1. **Conduct a Purpose Alignment Audit**
   List all your current commitments. Ask: does this serve my mission or someone else's?

2. **Create a Brand Boundaries List**
   Write down what aligns with your brand and what doesn't. Be clear and unapologetic.

3. **Invest in the Right Coach**
   Choose someone who will help protect your brand, amplify your message, and sharpen your focus.

4. **Write a Personal Brand Declaration**
   One sentence that sums up who you are, what you stand for, and what you deliver. Say it before every meeting, event, or partnership.

5. **Turn Pain into Power**

   Use your lessons as leverage. Tell your story. Build a program. Create a platform that empowers others who may be silently giving their power away.

You are not behind. You are being prepared. The detour was part of destiny. Let the $20K be your testimony, not your tombstone. Your purpose is waiting—and it's time to answer the call.

About The Author

Barbara J. Beckley is the CEO and Founder of DFN Broadcast Studio, a premier platform dedicated to helping entrepreneurs, thought leaders, and professionals amplify their visibility through TV streaming and media. As a seasoned Visibility and Purpose Strategist, international speaker, and 12X best-selling author, Barbara empowers individuals to share their stories, build their brand authority, and create a lasting legacy through media exposure. Her mission is simple yet powerful: help people unlock their voice and shine on global stages.

Tinyurl.com/BarbaraJBeckley

Facebook: Diamond Factor Network | LinkedIn: Barbara J Beckley | YouTube: Diamond Factor Experience Network

Chapter 18

Success Starts Where Survival Ends
By: Erin Baker

I can say, without exaggeration, that the best thing that ever happened to me was a nervous breakdown—followed shortly by getting fired.

Sounds wild, right?

But that moment—the collapse, the unraveling—was actually the beginning of everything I truly needed.

Let me give you three lenses to view this story through, because this is not just about me. First, I'm a single mom and an entrepreneur, navigating the world with ADHD, autism, anxiety, depression, PTSD, and a few other diagnoses that color my life. Second, this is a story for anyone who's neurodiverse, who's ever masked or molded themselves to survive. And third, this story belongs to everyone. No matter your background, gender, diagnosis, or life path—there's something here for you.

Before it all came crashing down, I had what looked like a very stable life. I had my master's degree, a 13-year career in higher education, a respected title, and a reputation as someone dependable, knowledgeable, and effective. I was also a single mom to a teenager with ADHD, autism, and anxiety. I was juggling, surviving, managing.

Until I wasn't.

The breakdown hit me like a freight train. I ended up in inpatient care, then intensive outpatient treatment. But what looked like a breakdown was actually burnout—autistic and ADHD burnout—set off by trauma and years of trying to be everything to everyone.

In therapy, I uncovered something deep and painful: toxic core beliefs that had shaped my entire life. I believed my value came only from what

I could do for others. I believed it wasn't okay to have needs. I thought rest was lazy and asking for help was weakness. No one had intentionally given me these beliefs—but I'd internalized them through years of culture, family dynamics, and institutional expectations.

Those beliefs were killing me.

So I started doing the work. Hard, relentless, soul-deep work. I had to deconstruct the framework that built my life and replace it with something new—something real. I had to learn how to be me.

That's when I realized: I didn't actually know who I was.

At 42, after years of studying neurodiversity to better support my son, I started recognizing the same traits in myself. ADHD. Autism. The pieces fit too well to ignore. Like many parents of neurodivergent kids, I had stumbled into my own diagnosis late in life.

As I looked back, I saw the constant masking—shapeshifting to meet others' expectations, earning value through achievement, fitting myself into spaces that weren't built for me. I'd been performing someone else's version of "acceptable" for decades.

The diagnosis wasn't the end of the story. It was the beginning.

Armed with this new understanding, I tried to create boundaries. I asked for accommodations. I tried to integrate healthier beliefs and advocate for myself in a system that wasn't built for people like me.

And that's when I got fired.

No, the paperwork didn't say "because you're autistic and have ADHD." But we both know that's what it was. The irony? I had been the resident expert on neurodiversity at that institution. Yet when I truly started living in that truth, instead of just teaching it, I became "too much."

But here's where the story flips again.

That firing? That burnout? That diagnosis?

It was freedom.

The safety of that job had become a cage. I was secure, but I was suffocating. Losing it all forced me to rebuild from a place of truth. For the first time, I asked: What do I want to create? Who am I when I stop performing?

And what I built was something extraordinary.

I became an entrepreneur—not because I had a business plan, but because I had a mission. A mission to help others redefine success on their own terms. A mission to support people—especially neurodivergent people—in building lives that actually work for them.

Here's what I've learned: every single person can be successful. But first, we have to reclaim the definition of success.

Success doesn't have to look like money, degrees, promotions, or a polished LinkedIn profile. For some, success means getting out of bed in the morning. For others, it means building something that reflects who they really are. Success is personal. And until we define it for ourselves, we can't achieve it.

So here's the roadmap I use—for myself and for others:

1. Define your success. Not society's version. Yours. What does a good day look like? What brings you peace? What fills you up?

2. Identify the barriers. This might include lack of support, unrealistic expectations, internalized beliefs, or environmental mismatches.

3. Address those barriers. This might take therapy, coaching, advocacy, or simply saying, "This system wasn't made for me—and I'm allowed to do it differently."

4. Identify your mindsets and beliefs. Which ones help you? Which ones hurt you? Change takes time, but awareness is where it starts.
5. Build support. No one thrives in isolation. You need people who see you, believe you, and will walk beside you.

6. Check in regularly. What's working? What's not? Celebrate even the tiniest wins.

7. Take action in small steps. Sustainable success isn't built in a weekend. It's built brick by brick, breath by breath.

None of this is magic. It's just real, intentional work grounded in truth.

For years, our systems—especially schools and workplaces—have treated people as if we're all the same. But we're not. We learn differently. We think differently. We are different. And that difference isn't something to be fixed. It's something to be honored.

When we truly meet people where they are, we stop asking them to fit the mold. We start building better systems around them.

That's what I'm doing now.

I help individuals—students, teachers, employees, leaders—reclaim their definitions of success. I teach people how they learn best. I advocate for systems that support diverse minds. I coach families and organizations through the process of change.

I started this journey in burnout, breakdown, and trauma.

Now I walk in truth, mission, and hope.

So, if you're in the middle of your own unraveling—if everything feels like it's falling apart—know this:

It might just be the beginning.

About The Author

I'm the founder and CEO of Baker Street Student Success and the "Turning Perfection into Authentic Happiness and Fulfillment" program. With over a decade of experience teaching students and educators, along with my personal background of managing autism, ADHD, and anxiety as both a former student and a parent, AND Having experienced my own nervous breakdown directly related to my perfectionistic tendencies. Now, I run my own coaching and consulting business, dedicated to empowering students, parents, and professionals to succeed, hopefully before the burnout or nervous breakdown.

Facebook| Instagram: Baker Street Student Success | TikTok: Baker Street Stud | LinkedIn: Erin Baker

Chapter 19

Never Can Say Goodbye
By: Dr. Tonya Fields
"A great soul serves everyone all the time.
A great soul never dies. It brings us together again,
and again." — Maya Angelou

I almost always laugh when comedians point out cultural differences between races. There seems to always be at least a grain of truth within the stereotypes, which makes the comparisons so comical, even on subjects as sad and devastating as death. One of my favorite social media personalities: @Hollywoodgengen (https://facebook.com/hollywoodgengen) dresses in drag as Ms. Renee and impersonates the dramatic behavior of "Aunties" at funerals. It is hilarious as he and sometimes some of his friends capture the attitudes and emotions of those paying their "final respects."

During a recent vacation, I shared a few of his skits with my family and very close friends, which prompted us all to share our personal wishes for our last celebration.
We all decided we wanted our farewell services to be filled with as much light and laughter as possible. My mother, one of the funniest people I know, said she wanted to be cremated, and she wanted no casket at her service. She wants us to have several glamor photos of her on display, and a party soundtrack mixed with hits of her favorite artist, and to make sure Prince songs played the most.

She wants everyone to take a few shots of tequila before, during, and after the service. My sister did not want any sad songs played; she wanted a happy vibe and even wanted us to play the popular dance song "Blow the Whistle" by Too Short at the service. I shared I don't want a funeral service at all and to only let a few select folks know that I even died—it shouldn't even matter to those who were not really a part of my normal existence.
Should anyone ask about me over the years, I want my loved ones to make up extravagant lies about trips I've gone on, such as away on a 6-

month cruise, or overseas on a shopping trip. For those whose lives I've touched, I request that they light a candle whenever they think of me and let the tiny flame be a reminder to do something nice for somebody. If there is a ceremony, make up tiny favor bags and give everybody a few of my favorite things, like a tiny bottle of Tabasco, a miniature Snickers candy bar & a travel-size bottle of Don Julio Reposado in memory of me. We each piled onto our stories, adding hilarious extras to make the service reflect our last wishes. No green beans at the repast!

We laughed until we cried until the reality of each other's death, as well as our own, became vivid and a bit too real, and suddenly it was no longer funny. Just joking about it was too much; the tears that collected in our eyes were no longer from laughter. Is there anything more painful than losing those you love the most or, even worse, seeing them suffer? If collectively we could appeal to God Almighty for significant changes for humanity, many rules surrounding pain and death would be at the top of the list.

The conversation became too much as we started talking about sad songs, the ones that make our hearts bleed even more. It doesn't matter who sings "Everything Must Change." I find it hard to choke back the tears. Songs by Boys II Men & Mariah Carey, Celine Dion, and dozens of other artists cause deep personal reflection, special memories, and fresh heartbreak that elicits the "ugly cry". We hugged each other longer than normal and made our way to our respective rooms to process the reality of each other's last farewell, and simply prayed it would be far off into the future.

We have so little control over death. The best we can do is to strive to show the people we love the best version of ourselves with every interaction. Expressing love and support during life is one of the few "controls" we have over death. We should "pay our respects" each time we interact because on any given day, we or someone we love just might join the "dearly departed." If we had known it would be the last time we saw or spoke to one another, or the last day we ever lived, what, if anything, would we have done differently? There are no "do-overs" or mulligans.

The last interaction with the deceased, no matter how exciting or mundane, loving or bitter, was the last time. Rarely are we ready for death; so often we think we have more time, but with each day that passes, we have less time.

When it is all said and done, it is the small, regular, everyday interactions that are the epitome of "Give them their Flowers". Even if you talk to someone every day, you can never really say "all that you wanted to say" should they pass away. Make time to visit, call, text, or send an old-fashioned letter or greeting card.

I feel blessed to assist someone who has an actual need or contribute to something that adds peace and joy to someone's life. Yet, most times, I feel some kind of way when contributing towards a funeral, even though I know the expenses are a necessary part of life. It took me a long time to realize that a funeral is not really about the deceased; rather, it is about the living who want to memorialize their life with as much grace, dignity, and love as possible.

My very special relative died while committing a crime. I am not judging their life, for we are all sinners. I did, however, give a side-eye to my relatives who wanted all of us to help pay for a horse-drawn carriage as part of his home-going service.

They even wanted to "Release the Doves" in honor of him. The "extras" seem to have given some in the family greater peace; however, it pissed the rest of us off to have to come up with the money. Side note: Some of the most important jobs in society are those associated with the death industry, so many of us are simply not cut out for it, especially me. Check out Comedian Kaution with Frazier Funeral Home www.facebook.com/ComedianKaution.

She does hilarious skits of daily situations dealing with families regarding preparing the body for funeral services. I wish she would run for Congress.

"We maintain a relationship with those who are no longer alive in the physical sense. Even though they have passed away, we treasure and hold on to the relationship..." — William Shatner

While preparing for this project, out of sheer curiosity, I ended up going down a brief YouTube rabbit hole, discovering information about various death and burial rituals around the world. The National Geographic provided several videos of documented rituals I had never heard of before, such as (1) keeping the body of the deceased at home for months or years; (2) digging the body up every few years and changing the clothes; and (3) turning of the bones. If you think you can stomach it, the video is 4:04 minutes, very high quality, and worth the click https://www.youtube.com/watch?v=hCKDsjLt_qUI.

I also invite you to watch an episode of The Unexplained: "Tales of the Dearly Departed" on the History Channel, narrated by William Shatner. After stumbling on those documentaries, I found the New Orleans "Jazz Funerals" and the Fantasy Coffins much less dramatic or bizarre. It is worth watching: https://www.youtube.com/watch?v=BEYK5Ki7jwM

With our days numbered, in effect, maybe we should all adopt a "hospice-like" mentality that expands across our entire life, not just when we get sick. Let us work to communicate love and encouragement and provide grace for one another's shortcomings and express our love to one another—all the time, as if it were the last time, because eventually it will be the last time.

The people I have lost have never completely left me. They still exist in my world, guiding me and loving me. I will never be ready to let them go. If I ever tried to let them go, I think I would die too, because I am me only because of each of them. Sending a special thank you to Jennifer Hudson for her song "Still Here" - I play it several times every year. I can feel them "still here with me all the time...".

Call to Action: Take Care of End-of-Life Business!
Suzy Orman, the popular personal finance expert, is hands-down my favorite financial advisor. I love her matter-of-fact, no-nonsense style. She advises everyone to prepare: (1) a revocable living trust, (2) a durable financial power of attorney, (3) an advance directive for healthcare, and (4) a will. She says, "Estate planning is an important and everlasting gift you can give your family."

There is an entire industry dedicated to the business of end-of-life planning and execution. There are now dozens upon dozens of helpful just-in-case binders and "checklists" available that store important directions, papers, policies, etc., to help guide our loved ones when we can no longer be a guide. The binders and workbooks have funny front covers like: "Crap, I'm dead, Now What?" or "Gone, But Still Telling You What to Do!" Let's commit ourselves to the serious tasks of providing ongoing support through legacy building and estate planning. If we do it right, we will live on through what we leave to others, even if it is only a personal letter that reminds those we leave behind that in our spirit, we never can say goodbye.

About The Author

Dr. Tonya Fields is the Founder and CEO of Connected Compass, an organization with goals to motivate, inspire, and empower college students with funding support, confidence, and skills needed to launch successful careers.

Dr. Fields is a U. S. Navy Veteran, with 25 years of service, retiring as an Information Systems Technician Master Chief. Her friends and family take pride in referring to her as "Dr. Master Chief". Her military background helped to develop her into a compassionate leader with a strong sense of empathy and compassion for others.

She is authentic, engaging and sincere. Dr. Fields holds a Bachelor's and Master's Degree in Computer Science from Norfolk State University and a Doctorate in Professional Studies in Computing from Pace University in New York. She serves as an Adjunct Professor and Cybersecurity Researcher at Norfolk State University. Her research interest has focused on Machine Learning for Natural Language Understanding used to build Artificial Intelligence models.

She is often quoted as saying "From the Hood to the Hood" to acknowledge her journey from growing up in the "*hood*" in the inner city of Grand Rapids, Michigan to her academic achievement of being "*hooded*" during her Doctoral ceremony.

Dr. Master Chief is a devoted wife of 21 years, mother of 6, and grandmother of 9. She invests in the community through her partnership with Melody Matthews and Associates, a real estate company dedicated to helping people find their way home and beyond.

www.connectedcompass.org

https://linktr.ee/Connected_Compass

Chapter 20

The Journey Continues — Biz Her Way

As you close the pages of this playbook, remember this truth: every woman's story, including yours, is still being written. The lessons shared here are from the triumphs and challenges of women and men who dared to build businesses

their way

are not just words on paper. They are blueprints for courage, resilience, and legacy. Whether you're taking your first step into entrepreneurship or expanding an empire, may this book remind you that success is not about perfection; it's about persistence, purpose, and the willingness to rise again and again.

But this is only the beginning. The *Biz Her Way* movement is more than a book; it's a community of women who are leading loud, building legacy, and creating impact together. I invite you to connect with me, the incredible authors who shared their journeys, and thousands of women around the world who are redefining what entrepreneurship looks like.

Join us at www.bizherwaysummit.com to stay part of the movement, attend our global summits, and be inspired by women who are changing the game in *Mind, Body, and Business.*

Your next chapter starts now. Write it boldly. Lead it your way— the Biz Her Way.

Sacha Walton, Founder of the Biz Her Way Movement

www.ingramcontent.com/pod-product-compliance
Lightning Source LLC
Chambersburg PA
CBHW070356200326
41518CB00012B/2257